THE PURPOSE OF THE CHURCH
AND ITS MINISTRY

THE PURPOSE
OF THE CHURCH
AND ITS MINISTRY

Reflections on the Aims
of Theological Education

By H. RICHARD NIEBUHR

IN COLLABORATION WITH
Daniel Day Williams and James M. Gustafson

HARPER & ROW, PUBLISHERS
New York, Evanston, and London

CONTENTS

FOREWORD

The following chapters on the nature and purpose of the Church, the ministry and the theological school constitute the first part of the report of *The Study of Theological Education in the United States and Canada*.

Hundreds of schools in the United States and Canada make it their business to educate men and women for the Christian ministry in Protestant, Roman Catholic and Orthodox churches. Their graduates form a large proportion of the three hundred thousand clergymen active in the numerous church organizations of North America. They work as pastors, preachers and priests, teachers and scholars, evangelists and missionaries, writers and editors, administrators of denominational, educational, social service and reform agencies, as chaplains in prisons, hospitals and military establishments. Doing splendid, indifferent or woefully inadequate work these ministers and the schools that train them are subject to praise and blame by themselves, the churches and the environing society. They are questioned and they question themselves. In this situation more than a hundred theological schools have agreed to examine themselves and the status of theological education in general, to raise immediate and ultimate questions about their purposes, their methods and their effectiveness in discharging their duties; to seek also ways of improving their own ministry. Under the leadership of the American Association of Theological Schools and with the financial support of the

Carnegie Corporation a study center was established to correlate the work of self-examination and to formulate its results.

The general reason for the inquiry is to be found, of course, in the conviction that "the unexamined life is not worth living"— a principle that has been given a special form in the Christian demand for daily and lifelong repentance. Institutions and communities no less than individuals are subject to this requirement. It is said that an uninspected army deteriorates and this is doubtless true of all human organizations. We tend to repeat customary actions unaware that when we do today what we did yesterday we actually do something different since in the interval both we and our environment have changed; unaware also that we now do without conscious definition of purpose and method what was done yesterday with specific ends in view and by relatively precise means. Education in general, and not least ecclesiastical education, is subject to this constant process of deterioration and hence in need of periodic self-examination.

Some special considerations have strengthened such general concern for self-study. The thought is abroad among theological educators and students that in the course of apparent repetition of traditional functions they have so adjusted themselves day by day to new pressures in the changing environment that they have lost the form and direction of inherited educational policy, so that the curriculum no longer is a course of study but has become a series of studious jumps in various directions. At the same time many of them are oppressed by the feeling that theological study does not sufficiently consider the changes that have taken place in human thought and behavior in the course of a revolutionary century. They note that in both respects they face problems similar to those that have led educators in other fields to undertake more or less promising reformations. Such examples have encouraged them to look forward to comparable efforts in the theological schools.

An even more significant occasion for theological self-examination lies in the temper of the times. In large sections of the Western world a new attitude toward theology and religion has become manifest. After a long period in which the need of many for a sense of life's meaning seemed to be supplied by the progress of civilization or by the realization of national destiny, disillusionment with the half-gods has made itself felt. Men who felt that they were born to die for the glory of nation or culture or for the sake of unborn generations or the advancement of knowledge, have been succeeded by generations who ask the ultimate questions with which religion and theology are concerned. Further, it is increasingly recognized by the thoughtful that the foundations of our civilization rest on deeper convictions than those generally acknowledged; that science and democratic life, literature and art, derive their ultimate orientation from religious faith; and that without renewal of the foundations the structure cannot endure. In this situation churches and theological schools sense that more is expected of them by their fellow men than they once thought and that they owe their neighbors more than they are prepared to give.

Moved by these concerns, in awareness of such needs, pastors and teachers of theology, administrators and boards of theological seminaries and now groups of these gathered loosely around a staff of inquirers with their advisers have undertaken for a brief space of time to examine their work and to ask large and small questions about its adequacy and improvement.

The subjects and objects of this study are, by and large, the

Protestant theological schools in the United States and Canada. The community of inquiry goes beyond these boundaries at certain points; it is narrower at others. Geographically it often extends beyond the United States and Canada since the questions and answers of theological educators and churches in Germany, England and France, Asia, South America and Africa, as overheard in the New World or as directly addressed to us here, enter into the discussion. Moreover, Christians can never forget that they are one people whatever the country of their residence. Again, the questions raised by Roman Catholic educators about their own schools and methods often run parallel to those of Protestants and their reflections are helpful to the latter. This is true also of the schools in which Jews carry on their theological work and educate young men to be rabbis. Primarily, however, those engaged in this particular inquiry are Protestants. First among them, again, are the institutions and men federated in the American Association of Theological Schools, but many schools not belonging to the association have co-operated freely. In general the group which has been drawn into the discussion has consisted of graduate schools of theology; but those who have been engaged in the task of correlating the inquiry have become very much aware that many nongraduate schools—among them Bible colleges and institutes—play a significant role in the educational venture and have a genuine interest in the outcome of theological self-examination. Various limitations have prevented the thorough study of this group of schools, but failure to draw them into the central community of inquiry does not imply any oversight of their significance.

No one can venture to speak for all those who have participated in the process of self-examination which has been focused for a little while in the office and the staff of *The Study of Theological Education in the United States and Canada*. All that is possible is that this small group should state in its own way the knowledge, reflections and convictions that have come to it in the course of an inquiry in which they have participated intensively for fifteen months. The members of the study staff—H. Richard Niebuhr, the director, Daniel Day Williams, the associate director, and James M. Gustafson, the assistant director—have visited more than ninety theological seminaries. They have had interviews with the deans of most of these schools and with scores of professors; they have met with more than forty faculties and have participated in regional conferences on theological education in Texas, California and Toronto. They have examined the publications of schools they were unable to visit. All but one of the schools of the American Association of Theological Schools and many nonmember institutions have supplied them with detailed information on organization, finances, enrollment, faculty, curriculum, et cetera. These reports have been studied and the statistical information has been analyzed. Thirty-six seminaries have given particular help by supplying information about their development during the last twenty years.

Considerable time has been devoted by the staff to the study of the American denominations, their ministries and interests in theological education. Denominational executives, particularly those charged with responsibility for the seminaries, have been most helpful in providing information and counsel. Members of the staff have participated in conferences of educators of the American Baptist Convention, the United Church of Canada, the Lutheran Church—Missouri Synod, the Disciples of Christ, the Presbyterian Church, U.S., and the Presbyterian Church,

U.S.A. With the the advice of denominational leaders and others
they compiled a list of pastors regarded by their colleagues as
"good ministers" and entered into correspondence with a number of them, chosen so as to make the whole group representative
of the denominational pattern. Thirty pastors gave their time for
personal interviews; conferences were held with groups of others.
A hundred members of the panel wrote reflective and illuminat-
ing letters about the purpose, limitations, opportunities and
hazards of the Protestant ministry and offered their counsel on
the improvement of theological education. In another phase of
the study intensive and repeated interviews were held with first-,
second- and third-year students at seven seminaries. Some of these
interviews were conducted by the assistant director, others by
members of the faculties. The reports—in some instances tape
recordings—of the interviews have been of great importance to
the staff in its efforts to understand how the various aspects of
theological education affect students. Among other things "field
work" was brought into a new perspective for them when it was
seen through the eyes of the young men and women. Conferences with students in some thirty schools supplemented the data
gained from interviews. Various limitations prevented the development of a program of consultation with Christian laymen.
The limited number of interviews held with representatives of
the business and academic communities and organized labor
were very enlightening, and reports of lay assessments of the
ministry made by other students of the subject were also helpful.

The data, insights and ideas gained from these sources and
from the study of many special documents have been worked
through by the members of the staff, individually and in many
seminar sessions. Now they venture to report on what they be-

lieve to have learned in the course of their study and attempt to state what they think is the main content and meaning of the long discussion that is going on among theological educators. On many matters of fact the statement can be relatively precise and objective. But when it deals with principles and aims it must undertake to set forth what has been variously expressed by many or has been only implicit in what others have communicated. In this respect the report cannot be "objective" but must remain a somewhat personal effort to clarify and organize ideas about Church, ministry and theological education that seem to be "in the air" or that seem to be developing in "the climate of opinion." This first volume, in particular, is necessarily an essay of this sort.

The whole report is to be issued in three relatively independent publications. The present book will be followed, presumably within the year, by a volume offering a more detailed study of the schools, faculties, students, curricula, et cetera. The third portion of the report is being published in a series of bulletins dealing with subjects requiring special emphasis or statistical tables too detailed for inclusion in the general volume. Of the former sort is the *Memorandum on the Theological Education of Negro Ministers* which appeared in September, 1955; of the latter sort, a study of trends in thirty-six representative schools from 1935 to 1955 which is now in preparation.

A further book, sponsored by the study but not written by members of the staff, is to be published soon. It will contain a series of essays on the history of the Christian ministry written by Church historians who have met in several conferences and submitted their manuscripts to one another so as to produce a genuine symposium. They are: Professors Roland Bainton of Yale University Divinity School, Edward Hardy of Berkeley

Divinity School, Winthrop Hudson of Colgate Rochester Divinity School, John Knox of Union Theological Seminary, New York, Sidney Mead of the Federated Faculty of the University of Chicago, Robert Michaelsen of the State University of Iowa School of Religion, Wilhelm Pauck of Union Theological Seminary, and George Williams of Harvard Divinity School.

There now remains the pleasant task of expressing publicly the gratitude of the directors of the study to the persons and organizations who have helped them in the inquiry. Among the scores and hundreds of these the following immediately come to mind: the chairman and members of the Executive and Administrative Committees of the American Association of Theological Schools who set the study in motion; the members of the Advisory Committee, The Reverend Theodore Ferris, Bishop Paul N. Garber, Reverend Ralph W. Loew, President Franc L. McCluer, President Walter N. Roberts, Professor Lewis J. Sherrill, Dean Charles L. Taylor, Jr., Reverend Gordon M. Torgersen; the presidents and deans of seminaries who gave their time and counsel liberally, and cheerfully answered irritating questionnaires; the denominational executives, secretaries of education, of departments of the ministry, and the secretaries of the National Council of Churches who advised us in many matters; the ministers who gave precious hours for interviews and letters; Professor Samuel Blizzard of Pennsylvania State University and Union Theological Seminary in New York who shared with us some of the preliminary results of a study of the ministry he is carrying on under the auspices of the Russell Sage Foundation; Marcus Robbins, the comptroller, and other officials of Yale University who administered the funds; Dean Liston Pope of the Divinity School of Yale University who provided ample and pleasant quarters for the office of the organization and supported it in many other ways.

All these and many others have made greater contributions than the study staff has been able to appropriate and to transmit. The defects of the report are not due to any failures on their part but are chargeable to the director.

Special thanks are due to the Carnegie Corporation of New York which made the study possible through its grant of sixty-five thousand dollars, and to its vice-president James A. Perkins whose interest in the project and whose counsel were constant sources of strength. The Carnegie Corporation, it should be said, is not the author, owner, publisher or proprietor of these or of the other publications issued by the staff of The Study of Theological Education in the United States and Canada, and is not to be understood as approving by virtue of its grant any of the statements made or views expressed therein.

Particular acknowledgment must be made of the work of those members of the staff whose names do not appear on the title pages of its reports. Robert Gessert, now of Smith College, rendered important service during the summer of 1955 in collating and interpreting statistical material. Mrs. Miriam C. Smith brought considerable experience in research and high competence to her work as secretary. Mrs. Fleur Kinney Ferm, the staff secretary, has worked on this project longer than any other member except the director. Her good judgment, skill and patience have made contributions to the study which though they remain unidentified are conspicuous to her associates.

Finally, the director must take this occasion to express his great gratitude to his colleagues, Professor Daniel Day Williams, now of Union Theological Seminary in New York, and Professor

James M. Gustafson, now of the Divinity School of Yale University, for their faithful comradeship in service and for the deepened understanding of Church, theology and education he gained from them. Their contributions to the present essay are much greater than can be indicated on the title page. The book is the result of a co-operative effort, though in the end one member of the group needed to develop and formulate the "sense of the meeting." He, therefore, must accept responsibility for the inadequacies and errors of the interpretation.

H. RICHARD NIEBUHR, *Director*
The Study of Theological Education
in the United States and Canada

THE PURPOSE OF THE CHURCH
AND ITS MINISTRY

CHAPTER 1

The Church and Its Purpose

I. THE CONTEXT OF THEOLOGICAL EDUCATION

When teachers examine themselves and their schools for the sake of discovering how to overcome difficulties or how to improve their work they are quickly led to ask far-reaching questions about the nature and the purposes of education. And in the course of that inquiry they quickly discover that education is so closely connected with the life of a community that queries about the aims of teaching and learning cannot be answered unless ideas about the character and the purposes of the society in which it is carried on are clarified first of all. This was illustrated a few years ago when President Harry S. Truman appointed a Commission on Higher Education which later issued its report under the title *Higher Education for American Democracy* and began its discussion with definitions of the dogmas and the goals of democratic society. Similarly a Harvard committee appointed to explore the basis for the reorganization of college teaching was instructed to concentrate on the *Objectives of a General Education in a Free Society*. No other approach to an educational problem seems possible, since a school is never separable from the community in which it works, whose living tradition it carries

1

on, into which it sends citizens and leaders imbued with that tradition and committed to the social values. Moreover, being itself a part of the community the school expresses the common purposes directly. In democratic society it values every individual and maintains academic freedom; in genuinely aristocratic society it seeks to cherish and nurture the excellent persons and to maintain their leadership. Of course the school also usually finds itself involved in the conflicts and confusions of purpose that appear in society.

It may seem that professional schools are an exception to the rule; that social context and purpose need to be considered only in the case of so-called "general education." Studies of medical, legal, engineering and theological education, unlike the inquiries referred to above, frequently ignore the community and raise few questions about social purposes. There are books on legal education in which such words as "nation" and "justice" rarely occur; studies of medical education that scarcely mention "health" and make no allusions to its place in a social system of values; discussions of theological education which seem almost studiously to avoid references to the Church or even to God and neighbor. Doubtless it is often necessary to abstract special from general purposes, and immediate from ultimate problems if progress is to be made toward overcoming irritating difficulties. But it is equally necessary, particularly at critical junctures, to attend to the wider context of special problems and short-range goals. For two reasons this appraisal of immediate against ultimate ends is necessary in theological education today. In the first place such education, now as always, is concerned with the nurture of men and women whose business in life it will be to help men to see their immediate perplexities, joys and sufferings in the light of an ultimate meaning, to live as citizens of the inclusive society of being, and to relate their present choices to first and last decisions made about them in the totality of human history by Sovereign Power. It would be anomalous were an educational work directed toward such an end not under the necessity of considering itself in the same light, of living in such a universal community and of relating its decisions to first commandments and final judgments. In the second place, theology, as expression, understanding and criticism of the life of faith, is today, like that life itself, in a critical situation. At least in many parts of Christendom the quest for meaning, the revival of historic religious convictions about man's nature and destiny, about his lostness and his salvation, and the need to realize the significance of these convictions in relation to contemporary world and life views, have led to a renewal of the theological endeavor. In school and pulpit theology today is not simply an affair of translating ancient ideas into modern language, but of wrestling with ultimate problems as they arise in contemporary forms. It carries on its task in continuity with a great tradition and on the basis of convictions implanted historically into historical men; it works in a community that has a structure and a definable faith. Nevertheless it functions in a situation where many, though not all, things are fluid; education for the ministry must take place in this situation. Under these circumstances it seems imperative that churchmen considering their task in educating men for the work of the Church take their general bearings and try to state in what large context, with what definable orientation, they are going about their task.

To be sure, there are those who argue that the reform of theological education cannot wait on the reformulation of theology.

The latter process is likely to be a long one and in the meantime many immediate questions must be answered. Whatever the fundamental problems of theology are, and whatever lines of inquiry may turn out to be most fruitful, the present curriculum is overloaded and the student must be relieved of some of the burden. Whatever the function of the ministry is, theologically considered, ministers must preach, organize churches, counsel the distressed, teach the immature, and they need to be trained by practice for the exercise of these functions. Whatever the Church ought to be, it is expected of schools that they furnish men well prepared to carry on the kind of work demanded of ministers by churches as they are. Again, it seems clear that many more or less technical questions of education cannot be answered theologically. Psychology of learning; social analysis of the societies in which students will work; statistical methods applied to the economic facts of ministers' salaries and the cost of tuition, and the like; and many other relatively precise procedures applied to limited data can give guidance to perplexed administrators that no amount of hard thought about the large question of man's life before God will yield. Those who urge these considerations upon us are plainly justified in criticizing procedures that begin only with questions about ultimate contexts and final goals.

Yet it remains true that if educational questions cannot be answered theologically, neither can theological questions be answered by use of the techniques of social or behavioral sciences however relevant the insights derived from these sciences may be to theology. The situation in theological education is comparable to the one in which every minister finds himself daily. When he deals with a mentally disturbed person he cannot take the place of the psychiatrist, but neither can the psychiatrist take his place;

when political issues are involved, he cannot fulfill the functions of the statesman, but neither can the statesman, as statesman, illuminate a civil crisis by bringing only ultimate perspectives to bear on it. Similar ambivalences characterize every human situation; ultimate and immediate concerns, long- and short-range goals, big and little questions, theological and technical perspectives are involved in it. The approach can never be from one direction only. No simple inductive or deductive procedure is sufficiently fruitful. Yet various approaches can meet; various efforts to understand can support each other as well as be at cross-purposes. When the question is one about the education of the ministry it will not do to ignore either the general—the theological— nor the particular—the educational—approach; the theologian as educator or the educator as theologian cannot carry on his theological and his educational critiques separately and independently, nor can he reduce them to one inquiry with one method in the hope of gaining one single answer.

II. DENOMINATION, NATION OR CHURCH?

Under these circumstances we must ask and answer questions about the social context of theological education and about the objectives of the society while we also define special problems and seek their solution. The general question is: What is the community in which the theological schools carry on their work and which they in part represent? Corollary to this is the question about the objectives of the community which the school will serve directly and indirectly.

The first, superficial impression is that the Protestant theological schools in the United States and Canada do not consciously count themselves members of one community but function as though they were responsible to many different societies. They are all "church schools" rather than state institutions in distinction from many European theological faculties; but the word "church" may mean denomination. Most of the seminaries seem to function within the specific context of that peculiar American order of church organization, the denomination. Their very number indicates that other reasons than the desire to perform an effective task in a single community have led to their establishment and maintenance. While some ninety medical schools seem sufficient to supply the United States and Canada with well-trained physicians twice as many theological schools, besides Bible colleges and institutes, are at work in these nations to educate ministers. In their control, in the statements of their objectives, in the composition of their faculties, these seminaries for the most part reflect their dependence on, and their loyalty to, denominations. The context in which theological education is going on is the baffling pluralism of Protestant religious life in the United States and Canada.[1]

Yet despite their number, their denominational affiliation and their service of denominational purposes the theological schools usually give evidence of sharing in a community of discourse and interest that transcends denominational boundaries. And this is

[1] The pluralism is somewhat less characteristic of Canada than of the United States. The *Ninth Census of Population* in Canada lists 28 religious groups, whereas the last published (1936) census of *Religious Bodies in the United States* listed 256 denominations and the 1956 *Yearbook of the Churches* 254. The numbers are not quite comparable, however, since in the Canadian census some of the group evidently include several separately organized bodies.

true of the denominations themselves. What then is this common life in which schools and denominations participate? One is tempted to define it as American or Canadian national existence or—since the schools in the two nations have much in common—as "the free society" or as "Western democracy." Something is to be said in favor of the suggestion. The separation of Church and state and the legal recognition of the principle of religious liberty in both nations have led not only to pluralism through the protection of established religious groups and the encouragement of spontaneity and inventiveness; but have also fostered voluntarism in church organization and made the clergy largely dependent on lay support. Churches so thrown on their own resources have become responsible to the felt needs of the people to an unusual degree. Spontaneity and the need for adaptation in a competive situation have helped to give them a popular, "grass-roots" and sometimes vulgar character that removes them a long way from establishments which still bear the traces of historic alliance with privileged classes. They have had to learn the arts of popular appeal and business efficiency. So they and their schools have come to be very much alike; they seem to be the religious representatives of the American societies.

An English theologian, well-acquainted with the American religious and theological scene, has remarked on these and similar characteristics:

I suppose that the strongest impression that the visitor from this country receives is of the immense vitality and vigour of American Church life. In this the Churches do but share in the vigour and vitality of American life generally. They seem to be an integral part of the American "way of life"—a vague phrase, but one which does signify something to the feelings of Americans even if hard to analyze in terms and propositions. This is perhaps one reason (only one) why a much larger proportion of the population are attached to Churches, and "go to Church," than in this country. It is a "done thing," not as mere adherence to accepted conventions, but as flowing spontaneously from the "Volk" or community levels of consciousness. One result of this vigour and vitality, this sense of being integrally one with the movement, drive and energy of the community generally, is the admirable efficiency with which, on the whole, the Church organization is run, an efficiency which is made possible by, and itself helps to make possible, a sufficiency of funds for the purpose. I will not say "business" efficiency, for that might be taken to imply a derogatory value judgment which I do not intend: nevertheless it *is* the counterpart in Church life (there is no reason why there should not be such a counterpart) of the business efficiency which on the whole does characterise the secular side of American life generally. As organizations American churches strike one as being on the whole marvellously well run. There throbs through them the mighty pulse of American life; and it is a very American pulse.

In other ways also the churches in the New World seem to be "American" or "democratic" and to participate primarily in the common life of the "free society." The pluralism of denominationalism seems to be a reflection of the pluralism of democracy. When we think of the overchurching of hamlets and cities, or of the great varieties in training and ability among the ministers, or of the regional character of theological schools, or of any other manifestation of this religious heterogeneity, and then look for a parallel or parable that will make this confusion somewhat intelligible we are led to think of the form in the formlessness of economic and political activity in New World democracy. We cannot helpfully compare this "church-system" to the school system or this Protestant ministry to the profession of medicine.

The "church-system" looks more like the "filling-station system," and the clergy in their varieties of responsibility and excellence seem most to resemble democratic political leaders—from town selectmen to governors, from demagogues to statesmen, from ward heelers to national party leaders. The unity present in this diversity is like the unity in the diversity, rivalry and tension of democratic political and economic life.

Yet the principle of unity in this Protestantism is not the democratic principle. Despite the American and democratic character of Protestant churches and the theological schools that serve them, an interpreter who tried to understand them primarily in this context would need to do violence to them, to twist the meaning of their affirmations of purpose and to misconstrue the character of the work that goes on in them. Canadian and American, denominational and sectarian as they are in coloration, in function and objective they are churches and their schools are church schools. The community in which they work is the Church; the objectives they pursue are those of the Church. Only one among the schools, and that one unofficially and incidentally, refers in its statement of purpose to "the American way of life." About half of them, to be sure, define their purpose by reference to a denomination which they serve. However, the other half do not mention denominational ties, and even those that do so rarely name the special organization without referring to a wider Church of which the denomination is a part.[2]

[2] The following statements are somewhat characteristic of such schools: Bethany Theological Seminary affirms that its object is "to promote the spread and deepen the influence of Christianity by the thorough training of men and women for the various forms of Christian service, in harmony with the principles and practices of the Church of the Brethren"; Augustana

What is true of the schools is true of the denominations in general, though one cannot escape the impression that both schools and parish ministers are often less intent on peculiarly denominational objectives and more disposed to think of themselves as first of all responsible in the whole Church for the work of the Church than are many denominational executives. This is not to discount the importance and value to them of their denominations. Few preachers or teachers feel that they can work in the Church, or have loyalties in it apart from work and loyalty within a particular order. But it is to say that they are concerned with the function of the *genus*—the theological school or the Christian ministry—and that the function of the species—the American or denominational school and ministry—is of subordinate significance to them or at least to increasing numbers of them. It is to say further that they tend to be more aware of the temptations which arise for them as members of the species than of those which come to them as representatives of the genus. Not a few, while rejoicing in the vigorousness of that "American way" of church life which the English visitor comments on, also accept his warning when he follows his statement about the "business efficiency" and popular character of Christianity in America

---

Theological Seminary "prepares students for the ministry of the Evangelical Lutheran Church with the special needs of the Augustana Church in view"; the charter of Berkeley Divinity School begins, "Whereas sundry inhabitants of this state of the denomination of Christians called the Protestant Episcopal Church have represented by their petition addressed to the General Assembly, that great advantages would accrue to said Church, and they hope and believe to the interests of religion and morals in general, by the incorporation of a Divinity School for the training and instructions of students for the sacred ministry in the Church aforementioned."

with reflections about its dangers. This "very American pulse" that beats in these church organizations, he believes,

inevitably and unconsciously affects the minister's apprehension of, and attitude to, his task, as it does also those of the theological student. The latter is apt to be rather more aware of himself as primarily a person being professionally trained to fulfill a key-office, as an administrator, executive and leader in a vast and important department of the community life of the American people, than as a man on whom God has laid an arresting hand calling him out of that life in the first instance in order to be sent back into it on that basis to a ministerial and prophetic task. This unconscious approach is perhaps fostered to some extent by the great emphasis placed in the seminary curriculum on "practics," and by the comparison I have not infrequently heard drawn between the minister's training and that of the medical man; that the former's work springs from, and is sustained by, a deep and continuous interior transaction with God, is apt to be somewhat overlooked.

As for the temptations which arise out of the denominational organization of the Church, warnings against them are frequent; many ministers, students and teachers become restive when the primacy of denominational loyalties is urged upon them. The denominational-interdenominational type of church organization is doubtless with us to stay, rooted as it is in the history and structure of North American life. But as its modification by means of institutional arrangements for co-operative work constitutes an enduring concern of American churchmen, so efforts to transcend the provincialism to which it tempts ministers and seminaries constitute a striking feature of the contemporary religious scene. Denominational organization and American life are both conditioning elements in the work of the ministry and of the theological schools; from them the latter derive both strength and weakness. Yet the primary context in which the ministry and theology do their work is neither denomination nor nation but the Church in its wholeness.[3]

Certain direct evidence of this sense of context is given in those academic statements of purpose to which reference has been made. Either in connection with some mention of their purpose to train men for a denominational ministry or without such allusion, the theological schools tend to define their objective in such phrases as these: "spreading and deepening the influence of Christianity"; promoting the "interest of religion and morals"; "training Christian leaders who are wholeheartedly committed to Jesus Christ and able to share his gospel in all its relevance through the Church and all agencies of God's kingdom"; "to provide leaders capable of bringing to others the saving

[3] The lively interaction of denominational and catholic interests in many theological schools with accompanying enthusiasms and tensions makes a variety of interpretations of the situation inevitable. A member of the Advisory Committee, commenting on this section of the report, writes: "When you write of the denominational seminaries you seem to fail to grasp the ecumenical spirit that characterizes so many of them. This fact of the ecumenical spirit in the denominational school is a tremendous thing with great possibilities for the future. It should be played up more." A colleague, however, comments: "My one question of emphasis concerns the characterization of the schools as accepting the 'whole Church' and an ecumenical context as their real base of operations. . . . I think the denominational tensions are a little more pervasive and difficult than you seem to suggest. . . . There is still a long way to go." The slight modifications and qualifications which have been made in the essay as a result of such comments, have been made in the direction suggested by the second critic. The "ecumenical spirit" in the schools today is indeed remarkable but the distance still to be traversed is more impressive than the distance covered.

knowledge of God in Christ Jesus"; "training leaders competent in this age to interpret truth and to direct activities of the Church in its related institutions at home and abroad"; "the preparation of men for the ministry of the Word and the sacraments." The schools work in the context of the Church even though they do not frequently mention that fact. They may not be as conscious of the Church as they are of its objectives, yet when they serve the latter they participate in the life of the whole Church and are moved out of the confines of sectarianism. Their libraries are neither highly denominational nor highly American or Canadian. The denominational "Fathers" doubtless have a place on many shelves and lists of reserve books, but it is also the ambition of every destitute librarian to acquire a set of Migne's *Patrologia* (it will have at least several kinds of symbolic value); and writings of the Protestant "Fathers" as well as of their sons, almost irrespective of denomination, are everywhere to be encountered. Wherever the theological student is at work he is challenged—at very least by those most catholic of teachers, the competent librarians[4]—to enter into conversation with a continuous if not identical group of thinkers. To an increasing extent Eastern Orthodox and Roman Catholic theologians are included in that company.

The courses of study in denominational as well as interdenominational schools are even more indicative of their participation in the common life of the whole Church. Wherever they are

[4] It is not implied that all theological librarians are competent any more than all the members of other faculty groups are so. But a heartening sign in the present situation is the increase of interest among these librarians in their work as teachers and the increase of concern among faculties for the development of school libraries as teaching centers.

being taught, by whatever methods and with whatever preconceptions, theological students are everywhere being asked to enter into long and serious conversations with the persons and communities of the Old and New Covenants of the Bible. The emphasis may be on the Word of God to men through that book ("Thus saith the Lord"); or on the words of men to God ("Out of the depths have I cried to Thee"); or on the words of men to men about God ("Him whom you ignorantly worship I proclaim to you"). But whatever the emphasis, theological students in classroom, study and chapel are introduced to the great historic reasoning of God with men and led to participate in it. It is not to be denied that there are many contentions about proper methods of instruction, about the possibility of understanding the Bible without the use of Hebrew, Aramaic and Greek; and about its ultimate meanings. Yet it becomes clear to one who listens sympathetically and attentively to what is going on in the classes that there is a great common denominator among these conservatives and liberals, these strict and latitudinarian constructionists. There is more of the whole Biblical content in the thought of most "Fundamentalists" than "liberals" believe. Not only Genesis 1 and Matthew 1 but Isaiah 40 and I Corinthians 13 are inscribed in their minds and hearts. Conversely there is far more Biblical knowledge and conviction in the liberal mind than ultra-conservatism imagines.

General participation in a common life appears also in the extent to which church history forms a part of almost every theological curriculum and in the tendency to study it as a single history of one Church with many branches, subordinating the history of the denomination and even of Protestantism and of Christianity in America to the story of the whole Christian society. The community in whose history teachers and students find their orientation is wider then denomination or country. Here again there are variations. The teaching of church history is sometimes made the occasion for developing a sense of alienation from other groups rather than for developing a sense of unity. Like every other history, it is used at times to promote indoctrination in a peculiar tenet. Yet fundamentally and generally it is taught as church history.

In the study of theology proper the whole-church orientation of the schools may be less evident, yet differences are less of a denominational or national than of a party character. Conservative theologians, who were Presbyterians, are studied more widely in some seminaries belonging to new evangelistic groups than among the heirs of John Knox; modern theologians belonging to Lutheran churches, such as Aulén and Nygren, may be used more faithfully in an Episcopalian seminary than in many a Lutheran school less sympathetic to Lund. With a few exceptions teachers and students do not engage in a denominationally restricted discussion but participate in a Protestant and a Christian conversation or debate about the ultimate problems of faith and life. In the so-called practical fields the unity is even greater; here there is common concern for developing relevant, effective preaching in the local church on the basis of Scriptures; for a religious education Christian rather than either humanistic or denominational in character; for guiding men into pastoral work that meets human needs.

Other factors in theological education also point to this participation in a common life. Important among these is the work of the interdenominational schools, staffed by members of many denominations, necessarily teaching church rather than denominational doctrine, history and practice. They are attended by students coming from many church groups who return on graduation to their denominations. While these schools supply only about 15 per cent of each years's B.D. graduates they represent American Protestantism to a larger extent than such numbers indicate. A large proportion of the teachers in the denominational seminaries has had its doctoral training in these schools; and a considerable number of widely read theological treatises come from the pens of their scholars. In such schools and elsewhere the supradenominational and supranational character of theological education is also significantly indicated by the increasing enrollment of students and the employment of teachers from other areas of Christendom.

Thus implicitly and explicitly the denominations in their concern for the education of ministers, and the schools entrusted with the task, make it evident that they think of themselves increasingly as branches or members of a single community, as orders and institutions with special duties or assignments to be carried out in partnership with other branches of one society. The idea of *Una Sancta*, of One Holy Church, is very pervasive despite relatively rare expression. There are exceptions; denominations and even more frequently small parties in them, contend for the sole validity of a particular form of creed, organization or liturgy.[5]

[5] One school characterizes its attitude toward other denominations as "magnanimous"; another recognizes only two church bodies—one of these in Europe—as soundly Christian; some denominational programs for the development of theological education move easily from praise of the ecumenical spirit to exclusive concern for the advancement of the denominational ministry. Catholic interest in the whole Church does not always lead to radical change of the denominational mind.

Rivalries and contentions also exist. Sometimes these are reminiscent of the tensions to be found in the relations of states and provinces to nation as a whole, sometimes to the more acerbic dissensions among the branches of the armed forces, all equally pledged to the defense of the country; sometimes they seem very similar to the tensions found among Roman Catholic religious orders; sometimes they seem like economic competition. In the permissive atmosphere of freedom apparently wild and individualistic doctrines flourish; new founders and new religions with new schools appear; false or true prophets rise in protest against established and bureaucratized organizations of religious life; zealous groups maintain that all others are out of step except their select company. But to the sympathetic observer the increasing unity of American Protestantism is more striking than its apparent diversity. He notes that the primary context of Protestant theological education in the United States and Canada is the Christian community in its wholeness. The contention for this orientation of thought and life continues indeed to go on in many a school and poses for it its deepest problems; but the movement toward participation in the universal Church is the dominant one.

III. TOWARD A DEFINITION OF THE CHURCH

The definition of the Church—even the awareness of its actuality—constitutes one of the main concerns of modern theology. Thus we have arrived at one of those points where the reform of theological education apparently must wait on the reformulation of theology. Much confusion and uncertainty in theological schools today seems to be due to lack of clarity about the community—the Church; about its form and matter, its relations and composition. Without a definition of Church it is impossible to define adequately the work of the ministry for which the school is to prepare its students. It seems impossible also to organize a genuine course of study including the Biblical disciplines, church history, theology, the theory and practice of worship, preaching, and education on other grounds than those of habit and expediency unless there is clarity about the place of these studies and acts in the life of the Church. It is impossible to achieve more than superficial correlation of studies in the history and philosophy of religion, in psychology and sociology, with the older disciplines, unless the relations of the Church to religion in general, to the particular religions and to secular culture have been intelligibly defined.

The results of the inquiry into the nature of the Church in which theologians and churchmen are engaged today cannot be anticipated. The contributions on the one hand of Biblical, historical and systematic theology, of history, the sociology of religion and the theology of culture; and on the other, the practical experiments and experiences in ecumenical, national, municipal and parish organization of church life, will, one may hope, eventually be brought together in some kind of temporary historical synthesis. For the present the question what the Church is in act and potency, remains largely unanswered. The problem is new in many ways; at least it is posed in new forms at the present juncture of history. Thus questions about theological education which arise because of uncertainties in the conception of the Church may be due less to failure to maintain traditional conceptions than to a situation in which new implications of traditional ideas and new possibilities of historical institutions dawn on the horizon.

Nevertheless, we must try to take our bearings; try to formulate some of the nascent agreements about the character of that Church in which theological education goes on and for the furtherance of whose objectives the ministry is being educated. In his effort to state tentatively and in his own way such apparently dawning agreements the author of this essay must employ the method of polar analysis; that is, he must try to do justice to the dynamic character of that social reality, the Church, by defining certain poles between which it moves or which it represents. Such a method is the best one available to him.

By Church, first of all, we mean the subjective pole of the objective rule of God. The Church is no more the kingdom of God than natural science is nature or written history the course of human events. It is the subject that apprehends its Object[6]; that thinks the Other; worships and depends on It; imitates It perhaps; sometimes reflects It; but is always distinct from its Object. It is integral to the self-consciousness of such a subject that it distinguishes itself from its Object. Several things are implied in this understanding of the Church: negatively, the Church is not the rule or realm of God; positively, there is no apprehension of the kingdom except in the Church; conversely, where there is apprehension of, and participation in, this Object there the Church exists; and, finally, the subject-counterpart of the kingdom is never an individual in isolation but one in community, that is, in the Church. Development of these themes would require more space than the scope of the present essay permits.

[6] The objection that God is never object but always subject often arises from a confusion of the word "object" as meaning "thing" with "object" as meaning the Other toward which sensation, thought, appreciation, worship, et cetera are directed.

What seems important is the distinction of the Church from the realm and rule of God; the recognition of the primacy and independence of the divine reality which can and does act without, beyond and often despite the Church; and the acceptance of the relativity yet indispensability of the Church in human relations to that reality.

Definition of subject and object are correlative. What the Church is as subject cannot be stated without some description of the Object toward which it is directed. Though an object is independent of a subject, yet it is inaccessible as it is in itself. What is accessible and knowable is so only from a certain point of view and in a certain relation. The communal point of view and perspective of the Church, or, better, the kind of receptivity created in the Church, puts it into a relation to its Object and makes possible an understanding of it that is impossible to every other point of view. The Church is not the only human community directed toward the divine reality; its uniqueness lies in its particular relation to that reality, a relation inseparable from Jesus Christ. It is related to God through Jesus Christ, first in the sense that Jesus Christ is the center of this community directed toward God; the Church takes its stand with Jesus Christ before God and knows him, though with many limitations, with the mind of Christ. Secondly, in that situation there is made available to it, or revealed to it, a characteristic and meaning in the Object—the divine reality—unknown from other perspectives, namely, the reconciling nature and activity of a God who is Father and Son, and also Holy Spirit. Once more it becomes evident that the effort to define the Church involves us in many problems of theology into which we cannot enter in this connection. But certain implications of the historic and apparently necessary Trinitarian understanding of the divine reality on which the Church depends may be called to attention as important for the reorientation of theological education. One of these implications is that in the relative situation occupied by the Church its function is always that of directing attention to its Object rather than to itself. Another is the recognition that it is inadequate and misleading to define the church and the Object on which it depends in terms of Jesus Christ alone. It is indeed the Christian Church, but as the Church of Jesus Christ it is primarily a Church of God and so related to, while distinguished from, all other communities related to the Ultimate.

We need to define Church further by use of the polar terms "community" and "institution." A social reality such as the Church cannot be described by means of one of these categories only and much misconception of the Church results from such exclusive use. Popularly and even among churchmen the institutional Church may be so emphasized that there is little appreciation for the Church that does not come to appearance in organizations and rites. Of the two ecumenical movements in our time the organizational effort to develop world-wide institutions takes precedence in many minds over that spiritual, psychological, intellectual and moral common life, transcending all national boundaries, which seeks institutions through which to express itself. Or again membership in the Church is widely regarded primarily as a matter of participation in institutional forms and actions, less frequently as engagement in common thought, common devotion and worship, common appreciations. But the opposite error is also possible; a common life, vaguely defined by reference to a common spirit also vaguely described, is exalted at the expense of institutional forms.[7]

These errors are like those made when a nation is defined either institutionally as state, or as pure community by reference only to national "spirit" or a "way of life." But it seems clear that no community can exist without some institutions that give it form, boundaries, discipline, and the possibilities of expression and common action. On the other hand, no institution can long exist without some common mind and drive that expresses and defines itself in institutions. The questions whether Church is primarily institution or primarily community, or whether one of these is prior, are as unanswerable as similar questions about thought and language. There is no thought without language and no language without thought, yet thought is not language nor language thought. The Church as institution can preserve as well as corrupt the Church as community; it can express and define through word and deed the common mind as well as thwart the common spirit. The Church as community can enliven but also stultify the Church as institution. So it was in the case of the Nazi Christian community which twisted the meaning and eventually the forms of common Christian institutions; so it is also in the confusions of the Christian with the democratic community.

[7] An example of this may be found in Professor Emil Brunner's The Misunderstanding of the Church (Philadelphia, 1953). Professor Brunner writes: "The New Testament Ecclesia, the fellowship of Jesus Christ, is a pure communion of persons and has nothing of the character of an institution about it" (p. 17); to this "Ecclesia which is always . . . a dynamic reality and nothing more, the existing churchly institutions are related as means . . . externa subsidia—in very diverse ways and proportions" (p. 109). The Ecclesia . . . is no institution. Therefore the church can never be the Ecclesia either by purification or recreation" (p. 107).

The American and Canadian Church scene that we have sketched indicates how much institution and community belong together, yet how distinct they are. In part the realization of the Church community in the New World waits on the development of institutions able to give it form and wholeness; in part the institutionalization in denominations expresses the variety and unity characteristic of the community on this part of the planet.

To describe the Church as a community of memory and hope, sharing in the common memory not only of Jesus Christ but also of the mighty deeds of God known by Israel, expecting the coming into full view of the kingdom on earth and/or in heaven; to describe it further as the community of worship, united by its direction toward one God, who is Father, Son and Holy Spirit yet worshiped more as Father or as Son or as Holy Spirit in this or that part of the community; to describe it as a community of thought in which debate and conflict can take place because there is a fundamental frame of agreement and because there are common issues of great import—to do all this and the much more that needs to be done would be to essay the work of a large part of theology. It must be sufficient here to note that the schools which serve *in* the Church and serve the Church cannot abstract community from institution nor institution from community; nor can any churchman. One or the other of these polar characteristics of the social reality may be emphasized, but it cannot be defined without some reference to the other pole or served without some concern for its counterpart.

We must deal more briefly with certain other polarities in the Church's existence. Among these are the complementary yet antithetical characteristics of unity and plurality, of locality and universality, of protestant and catholic. The Church is one, yet also many. It is a pluralism moving toward unity and a unity diversifying and specifying itself. It is, in the inescapable New Testament figure, a body with many members none of which is the whole in miniature but in each of which the whole is symbolized. Every national church, every denomination, every local church, every temporal church order, can call itself Church by virtue of its participation in the whole; yet every one is only a member needing all the others in order to be truly itself and in order to participate in the whole. Without the members there is no body; without the body no members. Schools cannot prepare men to work simply in the whole Church but must equip them for particular service; yet they cannot do so unless they keep them mindful of the whole and loyal to it.

The Church is local and it is universal. Where two or three are gathered in the name of Christ there he is present, but all to which he points and all that he incarnates is present also. Among other things the universal Church is present, for Jesus Christ cannot be there without bringing with him the whole company of his brothers, who have heard the Word of God and kept it, who were not created without the Word. He is never present without the company of the apostles and prophets, the patriarchs and singers who speak of him; nor without the least of his brothers of whom he speaks. The localized Church implies the universal, but the universal no less implies the local; without localization, without becoming concrete in a specific occasion, it does not exist. The school which educates men for service in this Church cannot but focus their attention on the parish and the meeting; it cannot make them aware of the significance of parish or Sunday morning service unless it turns from the localized occasion to the universal community represented and adumbrated in the occasion.

The Church is protestant and catholic. This is not only to say that there is much historic Protestantism in those institutions called Catholic churches, and much historic Catholicism in the institutions called Protestant. It is also to say that the principle of protest against every tendency to confuse the symbol with what it symbolizes and the subject with the object, is a constituent element in the being of the community, even apart from the institutional organizations. The Church as the people of God, whether under the Old or the New Covenants, is always the party of protest against religion in the religious human world. It protests against every effort to bring the Infinite into the finite, the Transcendent into the immanent, the Eternal into the temporal. The only finite symbol of God it tolerates is the symbol of emptiness—the empty Holy of Holies, the empty tomb. But protest has no meaning apart from what is protested against. The Church cannot be protestant without being catholic. The principle of catholicity—as the principle of incarnation rather than the principle of universality—is as much an ingredient of churchliness as is the principle of protest. Unless the Infinite is represented in finite form, unless the Word becomes flesh over and over again, though only as oral preaching, unless the risen Christ manifests himself in the visible forms of individual saintliness and communal authority there is no human relation to the Infinite and Transcendent. Negative and positive movements—the one in rejection of all that is little because God is great, the other in affirmation of the apparently insignificant because God is its creator, redeemer and inspirer; the one away from the world that is not God, the other toward the world of which he is Lord— must both be represented where the Church exists.

The final polarity to be considered in this adumbration of the form and nature of the Church is that of Church and world. This is like the first polarity of subject and object insofar as it is not a polarity in the Church but one in which it participates as itself a kind of pole. The Church lives and defines itself in action vis-à-vis the world. World, however, is not object of Church as God is. World, rather, is companion of the Church, a community something like itself with which it lives before God. The world is sometimes enemy, sometimes partner of Church, often antagonist, always one to be befriended; now it is the co-knower, now the one that does not know what Church knows, now the knower of what Church does not know. The world is the community of those before God who feel rejected by God and reject him; again it is the community of those who do not know God and seem not to be known by him; or, it is the community of those who knowing God do not worship him. In all cases it is the community to which the Church addresses itself with its gospel, to which it gives an account of what it has seen and heard in divine revelation, which it invites to come and see and hear. The world is the community to which Christ comes and to which he sends his disciples. On the other hand, the world is the community of those who are occupied with temporal things. When, in its sense of rejection, it is preoccupied with these temporal matters it is the world of idolatry and becomes foe of the Church. When it is occupied with them as gifts of God—whether or not the consciousness of grace becomes explicit—it is the partner of the Church, doing what the Church, concerned with the nontemporal, cannot do; knowing what Church as such cannot know. Thus and in other ways the relations of Church and world are infinitely variable; but they are always dynamic and important. To train men for the ministry of the

Church is to train them for ministry to the world and to introduce them to the conversation of Church and world, a conversation in which both humility and self-assurance have their proper place.

If our interpretation of the spirit of the Protestant theological schools is in any way correct then it is Church defined somewhat in the foregoing manner that constitutes the society in which they function and whose objectives they serve directly and indirectly, consciously or unconsciously. Different schools and different denominations doubtless represent different perspectives and emphases in their understanding of this Church; yet they participate in the common life insofar as they respect and gain profit from each other's contributions.

IV. THE PURPOSE OF THE CHURCH: THE INCREASE OF THE LOVE OF GOD AND NEIGHBOR

What are the objectives of the Church? That they are many in number is clear from the statements of purpose made by schools when they define to what end they are training ministers, and by other church organizations—denominations, councils, conferences, et cetera—when they justify their activities. Some speak in individual terms of the cultivation of the Christian life or the salvation of souls; others state their goal to be the building up of the corporate life of the Church or of some part of it; again the goal is defined as the "communication of the vital and redeeming doctrines of Scriptures," or it is otherwise described by reference to the Bible as the ultimate source of all that is to be taught and preached. Elsewhere the end is defined as the preaching of the gospel and the administration of the sacraments; or, again, as the development of the life of prayer and worship. Perhaps most frequently the goal set forth is increase of belief in Jesus Christ, of discipleship to him and the glorification of his name. These multiple aims of churches and schools are again multiplied as one proceeds from grand statements about the purpose of the large organizations to the specialized goals of boards and departments, of courses and classes, of rural and urban congregations, of ministries of preaching and education and pastoral work and of preparation for such particular functions. The multiplicity of goals corresponds to the pluralism in the Church that is made up of many members, each with its own function; that stands in many relations to God, who is complex in his unity, and in many relations to a world protean in its attitudes toward God and the Church.

The question is whether there is one end beyond the many objectives as there is one Church in the many churches. Is there one goal to which all other goals are subordinate, not necessarily as means to end, but as proximate objectives that should be sought only in relation to a final purpose? When we deal with the complex activities of a biological organism or a person or a society the analogies of mechanical operation are misleading. The circulation of the blood, for instance, is not a means to the end of the functioning of the nervous system, nor is either a means only to the health of the body since that health also comes to expression in them. Still the healthy functioning of the whole body is in a sense a goal that a physician will have in view as he pursues the proximate end of improving circulation. The question of the ultimate objective of the whole Church and of the seminaries in the Church does not reduce questions about proximate ends to questions about means, but it poses the problem of the final unifying consideration that modifies all the special strivings.

Once more then we must venture to anticipate, though only in adumbrations, the answer to a question properly answerable only by the combined and continuous work of many theologians approaching the problem with the aid of many special studies and of many experiences. Such a statement will inevitably be somewhat private, yet though personal it is the report of what has been heard and understood in a conversation in which many contemporary ministers and teachers, many churchmen of the past and, above all, the prophets and apostles participate. As such a report it may gain some assent together with much correction and may be of some aid in moving forward the debate about the objective of the churches and their schools and in overcoming some current confusions.

The conversation about the ultimate objective is many faceted. It includes many interchanges on special issues through which, however, the movement toward the definition of the ultimate issue and the final objective proceeds. There is, as we have noted, a debate between those who define the last end of the Church individualistically as salvation of souls and those who think of it as the realization of the redeemed society. But extreme individualism and extreme emphasis on society are rare. Recognition of the social character of the individual and of the interpersonal character of society brings the parties somewhat closer to each other and both are challenged by the question: What is the chief end of man, whether as redeemed individual or redeemed community? Another debate, the one about Church and Bible, is leading, it appears, to somewhat similar results. Protestantism in general and particularly in

America is marked by devotion to the Bible; it often conceives its end to be the dissemination of Biblical truth and increase of devotion to Scriptures. Catholicism, on the other hand, tends to be church-centered and often finds its goal in the building and strengthening of loyalty to the Church. But the study of the Bible in Protestantism, with its demonstrations of the close relations of the people and the Book both in the Old and New Covenant periods, and historical theology with its reflections on the manner in which at different times the Church interprets Bible, bring Church and Scriptures into inseparable relations of mutual dependence. Moreover, in practice concentration on the Book is ultimately self-corrective since the Bible faithfully studied allows none to make it the highest good or its glorification the final end. It always points beyond itself not so much to its associate, the people, as to the Creator, the suffering and risen Lord and the Inspirer. This is true also of the Church; it loses its character as Church when it concentrates on itself, worships itself and seeks to make love of Church the first commandment. Tension and antagonism between Bible-centered and Church-centered members of the community is being ever-renewed but is also being evermore resolved and their debate is led to higher issues by the witness of the Bible and the Church themselves to that which transcends both. Another long debate has gone on in history and is alive today among those who agree that the chief end of the Church is to gain followers of Jesus Christ or to proclaim his Lordship. Christian humanism, present to a minor extent in denominations and schools, but widely prevalent in the "latent" church which seems large and important in America, is strong in its devotion to the Son of Man; reliance upon the Son of God is more characteristic of the ecclesiastical institutions and of the majority movement in the community. Yet exclusively Jesus-centered and exclusively Christ-centered groups contradict not only each other but also contradict Jesus Christ himself who will not bear witness to himself but to the one who sent him. The great central position of the historic Church maintains itself amidst these variations, affirming not only the actuality and unity of both human and divine natures, the identity of the historic with the risen Lord, but also some form of the Trinitarian conviction, which does not allow the separation of the Son of Man and Son of God, from the Father and the Spirit. Devotion directed toward Jesus Christ is at least partly redirected by him to the One he loves and who loves him, and to the world created and redeemed by the love of God. Nothing less than God—albeit God in the mystery of his being as Father, Son and Holy Spirit—is the object toward which Scriptures, Church and Jesus Christ himself direct those who begin by loving them.

Is not the result of all these debates and the content of the confessions or commandments of all these authorities this: that no substitute can be found for the definition of the goal of the Church as the *increase among men of the love of God and neighbor?* The terms vary; now the symbolic phrase is reconciliation to God and man, now increase of gratitude for the forgiveness of sin, now the realization of the kingdom or the coming of the Spirit, now the acceptance of the gospel. But the simple language of Jesus Christ himself furnishes to most Christians the most intelligible key to his own purpose and to that of the community gathered around him. If the increase among men of love of God and neighbor is the ultimate objective may it not be that many of our confusions and conflicts in churches and seminaries are due to failure to keep this goal in view while we are busy in the pursuit of proximate ends that are indeed important, but which set us at cross-purposes when followed without adequate reference to the final good?

Any adequate discussion of the theme of love of God and neighbor and of its relevance to Church and school requires all the resources of the theological curriculum from study of the Scriptures through systematic theology, the philosophy, psychology and history of religion, Christian and social ethics to pastoral theology, Christian education and homiletics. Yet in relative brevity some things can be said about this theme which, one hopes, will invite the assent of many members of the community, however great their dissent because of the incompleteness of the statement and because differences of emphasis are inevitable. The statement of a final end can never be a final statement until the whole community confesses it in the moment of its achievement.

In the language of Christianity love of God and neighbor is both "law" and "gospel"; it is both the requirement laid on man by the Determiner of all things and the gift given, albeit in incompleteness, by the self-giving of the Beloved. It is the demand inscribed into infinitely aspiring human nature by the Creator; its perversion in idolatry, hostility and self-centeredness is the heart of man's tragedy; its reconstruction, redirection and empowerment is redemption from evil. Love of God and neighbor is the gift given through Jesus Christ by the demonstration in incarnation, words, deeds, death and resurrection that God is love—a demonstration we but poorly apprehend yet sufficiently discern to be moved to a faltering response of reciprocal love. The purpose of the gospel is not simply that we should believe in the love of God; it is that we should love him and neighbor. Faith in God's love toward man is perfected in man's love to God and neighbor. We love in incompleteness, not as redeemed but in the time of redemption, not in attainment but in hope. Through Jesus Christ we receive enough faith in God's love toward us to see at least the need for and the possibility of a responsive love on our part. We know enough of the possibility of love to God on our part to long for its perfection; we see enough of the reality of God's love toward us and neighbor to hope for its full revelation and so for our full response.

In both law and gospel the love of God and the love of neighbor are inseparably related. Historically they are associated in Judaism and Christianity, in the two tables of the Ten Commandments, in the double summary of the law offered by Jesus, in apostolic preaching, in the theology and ethics of Catholic and Protestant churches. Despite tendencies in Christian history toward solitary union with God on the one hand and toward nontheistic humanitarianism on the other the unity of the two motifs has been vindicated many times. The inseparability of the two loves has been less manifest in theological analysis than in the actuality of history but theology has pointed out often enough how the thought of God is impossible without thought of the neighbor and how the meaning and value of the companion's life depends on his relation to God. With their understanding of the divine-human nature of Jesus Christ and of the ubiquity of Christ in all compassionate and needy companions, Christians are led to see that as the neighbor cannot exist or be known or be valued without the existence, knowledge and love of God, so also God does not exist as God-for-us or become known or loved as God except in his and our relation to the neighbor. The interrelations of self, companion and God are so intricate that no member of this triad exists in his true nature without the others, nor can he be known or loved without the others. If we substitute "Jesus Christ" for "neighbor" Christians in general will accept that statement; but there is danger in that substitution as well as the possibility of enlightenment, since the relation of Jesus Christ to our other neighbors is often obscured in theology; his revelation of what it means to be a man is often forgotten in favor of exclusive attention to his disclosure of what it means that God is, and is Good. Yet the latter illumination could not take place without the former.

God's love of self and neighbor, neighbor's love of God and self, self's love of God and neighbor are so closely interrelated that none of the relations exists without the others. The intricacy and unity of the human situation before God is not less dynamic and complex than the one we encounter in nature when we explore the energetic world of the atom or of a sidereal system. Yet we can only speak in succession of what appears in contemporaneousness; in discourse we must abstract relations, such as love, from the terms related and the terms from each other, so that we are always in danger of speaking of God without reference to the being he loves and that loves him; of speaking about religion or love of God as distinct from ethics or the love of neighbor. Such dangers must be accepted and faced; theology must be content to spend no small part of its energies in the correction of the errors which ensue from its necessary mode of working.

What then is *love* and what do we mean by *God* and by *neighbor* when we speak of the ultimate purpose of Church, and so of theological education, as the increase of love of God

and neighbor among men? By love we mean at least these attitudes and actions: rejoicing in the presence of the beloved,
gratitude, reverence and loyalty toward him. Love is rejoicing
over the existence of the beloved one; it is the desire that he be
rather than not be; it is longing for his presence when he is
absent; it is happiness in the thought of him; it is profound
satisfaction over everything that makes him great and glorious.
Love is gratitude: it is thankfulness for the existence of the beloved; it is the happy acceptance of everything that he gives
without the jealous feeling that the self ought to be able to do
as much; it is a gratitude that does not seek equality; it is wonder over the other's gift of himself in companionship. Love is
reverence: it keeps its distance even as it draws near; it does not
seek to absorb the other in the self or want to be absorbed by it;
it rejoices in the otherness of the other; it desires the beloved to
be what he is and does not seek to refashion him into a replica
of the self or to make him a means to the self's advancement. As
reverence love is and seeks knowledge of the other, not by way
of curiosity nor for the sake of gaining power but in rejoicing
and in wonder. In all such love there is an element of that
"holy fear" which is not a form of flight but rather deep respect
for the otherness of the beloved and the profound unwilling-
ness to violate his integrity. Love is loyalty; it is the willingness
to let the self be destroyed rather than that the other cease to
be; it is the commitment of the self by self-binding will to make
the other great. It is loyalty, too, to the other's cause—to his
loyalty. As there is no patriotism where only the country is
loved and not the country's cause—that for the sake of which
the nation exists—so there is no love of God where God's cause

is not loved, that which God loves and to which he has bound himself in sovereign freedom.

What, further, do we mean by the word God when we speak of the love of God? Not less than this surely—the Source and Center of all being, the Determiner of destiny, the Universal One—God the Father Almighty, Maker of Heaven and Earth. By God we cannot mean first of all love itself as the relation that binds all things together; the proposition that God is love cannot be converted without loss and error into the statement that love is God. Neither do we mean by God any lovely being easily made the object of our affection. We encounter no demand in ourselves or in our world to love that to which we are naturally attracted. Neither is there any promise or hope in the idea that we shall come to love with rejoicing, gratitude, reverence and loyalty, all that now easily arouses in us the movements of our desire. The movement of our love toward all these things, though they go by the name of God or gods, is the way of our idolatry; it is the movement toward the many away from the One, toward the partial instead of the universal, toward the work of our hands rather than toward our Maker. The demand and the promise refer to the One beyond all these.

The problem of man is how to love the One on whom he is completely, absolutely dependent; who is the Mystery behind the mystery of human existence in the fatefulness of its selfhood, of being this man among these men, in this time and all time, in the thus and so-ness of the strange actual world. It is the problem of reconciliation to the One from whom death proceeds as well as life, who makes demands too hard to bear, who sets us in the world where our beloved neighbors are the objects of seeming animosity, who appears as God of wrath as

well as God of love. It is the problem that arises in its acutest
form when life itself becomes a problem, when the goodness
of existence is questionable, as it has been for most men at
most times; when the ancient and universal suspicion arises
that he is happiest who was never born and he next fortunate
who died young.

Reconciliation to God is reconciliation to life itself; love to
the Creator is love of being, rejoicing in existence, in its source,
totality and particularity. Love to God is more than that, however, great as this demand and promise are. It is loyalty to the
idea of God when the actuality of God is mystery; it is the
affirmation of a universe and the devoted will to maintain a
universal community at whatever cost to the self. It is the
patriotism of the universal commonwealth, the kingdom of God,
as a commonwealth of justice and love, the reality of which is
sure to become evident. There is in such love of God a will-to-
believe as the will-to-be-loyal to everything God and his kingdom stand for. Love to God is conviction that there is faithful-
ness at the heart of things: unity, reason, form and meaning in
the plurality of being. It is the accompanying will to maintain
or assert that unity, form and reason despite all appearances.
The dark shadow of this love is our combative human loyalty
which in its love of gods—principles of religion, empires and
civilizations, and all partial things—denies while it seeks to affirm the ultimate loyalty and so involves us in apparently never-
ending religious animosities which at the same time unite and
divide neighbors, as they forge close bonds of loyalty to each
other in a common cause among closed societies disloyal to each
other.

Who, finally, is my *neighbor*, the companion whom I am

commanded to love as myself or as I have been loved by my most loyal neighbor, the companion whose love is also promised me as mine is promised him? He is the near one and the far one; the one beside the road I travel here and now; the one removed from me by distances in time and space, in convictions and loyalties. He is my friend, the one who has shown compassion toward me; and my enemy, who fights against me. He is the one in need, in whose hunger, nakedness, imprisonment and illness I see or ought to see the universal suffering servant. He is the oppressed one who has not risen in rebellion against my oppression nor rewarded me according to my deserts as individual or member of a heedlessly exploiting group. He is the compassionate one who ministers to my needs: the stranger who takes me in; the father and mother, sister and brother. In him the image of the universal redeemer is seen as in a glass darkly. Christ is my neighbor, but the Christ in my neighbor is not Jesus; it is rather the eternal son of God incarnate in Jesus, revealed in Jesus Christ. The neighbor is in past and present and future, yet he is not simply mankind in its totality but rather in its articulation, the community of individuals and individuals in community. He is Augustine in the Roman Catholic Church and Socrates in Athens, and the Russian people, and the unborn generations who will bear the consequences of our failures, future persons for whom we are administering the entrusted wealth of nature and other greater common gifts. He is man and he is angel and he is animal and inorganic being, all that participates in being. That we ought to love these neighbors with rejoicing and with reverence, with gratitude and with loyalty is the demand we dimly recognize in our purer moments in science and religion, in art and politics. That we shall love them as we do not now, that is the hope which is too good to be true. That we are beloved by them and by God, that is the small faith, less than the mustard seed in size, which since the time of Abraham and of Jesus Christ remains alive, makes hope possible, encourages new desire and arouses men to anticipated attainments of future possibility.

When all is said and done the increase of this love of God and neighbor remains the purpose and the hope of our preaching of the gospel, of all our church organization and activity, of all our ministry, of all our efforts to train men for the ministry, of Christianity itself.

V. CONFUSING PROXIMATE WITH ULTIMATE GOALS

Our efforts to define the context of theological education as the whole Church, and to describe its goal as the increase of the love of God and neighbor, have removed us a long way from the actuality of schools, churches and ministry in the United States and Canada. To be sure, these institutions reveal in various ways that this context and this goal are implied in what they do but they also make evident that very often they are not directly concerned about such apparently remote things. They usually speak of more proximate contexts and goals and often manifest an almost ultimate concern in less ultimate matters. From such confusions of the proximate with the ultimate arise some of their external and internal conflicts. Not all conflicts about proximate ends and immediate means are traceable to this source. Theological like every other type of education is involved, as has been noted, in a host of dilemmas that cannot be solved theologically; but its difficulties are increased tremendously by the internal conflict in which it is engaged when it substitutes the relative for the absolute.

Of these confusions the most widely criticized, though not the most important, is the confusion of a branch of the Church with the whole Church. The tendency to regard a denomination as the ultimate environment in which the school carries on its work or as at least the last society to whose purposes reference must be made is on the wane, as has been pointed out, in most of the seminaries and Bible colleges in the United States and Canada. But it is still strong in many places and one may expect that it will manifest itself in ever-new forms. Where it prevails theological education is necessarily provincial in character; it is neither theological nor educational, since it does not lead a student to any direct confrontation with the theological object nor induce him to participate in liberating dialogue with all companions directed toward that object. Against this tendency theology and faith will wage constant battle, though it is clear that no technical approach to curriculum construction or teaching method will enable any group to win this struggle and that no victorious party is secure against falling into the temptation to substitute a new form of this fallacy for the defeated one. That schools and churches so provincial in character and outlook make contributions despite themselves to the whole Christian movement is not to be gainsaid. Neither would one be justified in maintaining that a Church of undifferentiated wholeness and unity can exist or that the elimination of denominational differences would solve the underlying problem. The confusion between part and whole is not to be avoided by denying the reality of the parts but only by the acceptance of diversity and limitation and the corollary recognition that all the parts are equally related in the whole to the ultimate object of the Church. The denominational structure of the Church in the United States and Canada does not need to be eradicated before theological education can be put on a sounder basis, but a denominationalism that puts loyalty to the branch of the Church above all other loyalties involves theological education in internal self-contradictions that vitiate its work.

More significant today than the confusion of a branch of the Church with the whole Church is the confusion of Church, considered as whole or in its essence, with the ultimate context of theological education. Whether the term Church or the term Christianity is used, there is an internal contradiction in a theology and a Christian educational system that regard the work of the Church as the final activity to be considered. The confusion is a common one. It has become more prevalent in recent years since the fallacies of concentration on religion have become apparent. Not long ago religion was often credited with the power and grace that belong only to the God of faith; religion, it was said, inspired, healed and saved. Now that subjectivism is often replaced by another which puts the Church in the place of religion but confuses its work with that of its Lord and equates devotion to it with loyalty to the kingdom of God. The resulting confusion is similar to the one that appears in political life when a particular democratic society is made the object of a devotion that genuine democracy extends only to humanity, created free and endowed with natural rights prior to any recognition of these facts. In the case of Communism it has become plain what internal contradictions and perversions ensue when the promotion of the party is substituted for the pursuit of the party's cause. That substitution has led to all manner of corruption. Christianity and the Church have not been slow to criticize Judaism because in it the idea of a people chosen for service was often converted into the idea of a people chosen for privilege while the victory of the cause which the people was chosen to promote was frequently equated with the victory of the people. It is always easy to discern the mote in the eye of another. The beam in our churchly or Christian eye is not so easily seen. Both in thinking of the context in which we work in the Church and of the goal we pursue, it seems easy to accept and propagate the idea that the last reality with which we are concerned is the Church itself, and that the summary commandment we obey is to love Christianity with heart, soul, mind and strength. This exaltation of Church or of Christianity leads us then to an effort not to reconcile men with God or to redirect their love and ours toward God and the neighbor but rather to convert them to Christianity. These purposes are not more identical than subject and object are identical. It is one thing to be reconciled to God and to conceive some love for the neighbor and hence to participate in the community of which Jesus Christ is the pioneer and founder; it is another thing to take for granted that if one is brought into membership with the historical society called the Church love of God and neighbor will automatically ensue.

It is evident that in dealing with this confusion we are attending to a subject that is important not only to theological education but to all the work of the churches. The confusion of a proximate, churchly, with the ultimate, divine, context and the attendant confusion of goals, lies at the heart of many dilemmas in which the Christian missionary enterprise is involved in its dealings with the adherents of other religions. It is close also to the problems of Protestantism in its encounters with the Roman Church. Having begun with protest against tendencies in the latter branch of Christianity to regard the Church as the representative of God it has often succumbed to the same tendency itself. In consequence it has found itself engaged in competition on the same ground its rival occupies and using weapons which its own principles deny to it. But if the confusion is serious in all other areas of Church action it is not the less serious in theological education. When it prevails such education necessarily becomes indoctrination in Christian principles rather than inquiry based on faith in God; or it is turned into training in methods for increasing the Church rather than for guiding men to love of God and neighbor. The confusion of the subject with the subject's object is more than an epistemological fallacy.

A similar confusion to which Protestantism is even more prone ensues when the Bible is so made the center of theological education that the book takes the place of the God who speaks, and love of the book replaces devotion to the One who makes himself known with its aid. The problem of the relation of Scriptures to revelation, of the Word of God spoken through the prophets and incarnate in Jesus Christ to the living Word, is one that has greatly concerned theology especially since the days of the Reformation. It is of particular importance in contemporary discussion. But it is not necessary to await the outcome of a long debate before one arrives at the conclusion that whatever else is true about these relations, the identification of the Scriptures with God is an error, a denial of the content of the Scriptures themselves. To give final devotion to the book is to deny the final claim of God; to look for the mighty deeds of God only in the records of the past is to deny that he is the living God; to love the book as the source of strength and of salvation is to practice an idolatry that can bring only confusion into life. Without the Bible, as without the Church, Christians do not exist and cannot carry on their work; but it is one thing to recognize the indispensability of these means, another thing to make means into ends. There is much theological education that suffers from inadequate attention to the Biblical history of divine words and deeds; there is more that suffers from so close a concentration on these that the One to whom Scriptures bear witness is overshadowed by the witness. The lines between theological education and Bible study are hard to draw. Genuine Bible study is theological and genuine theology cannot succeed without Bible study. But there is a Biblicism that is not theological because it does not make God so much as Scriptures the object of its interest, and which depends for law and grace not on Father, Son and Holy Spirit but on Bible. This kind of Biblicism involves theological education as well as the churches in inner contradictions.

The most prevalent, the most deceptive and perhaps ultimately the most dangerous inconsistency to which churches and schools are subject in our time (perhaps in all the Christian centuries) arises from the substitution of Christology for theology, of the love of Jesus Christ for the love of God and of life in the community of Jesus Christ for life in the divine commonwealth. Once more we touch upon a problem with which theology in our time is deeply concerned, and which makes evident how much the reconstruction of theological education depends on the reconstruction of theology. Yet as in the case of Biblicism it is hardly necessary to await the outcome of many inquiries before concluding that substantial error involving many further confusions is present when the proposition that Jesus Christ is God is converted into the proposition that God is Jesus Christ. If the long story of the Trinitarian debate in Christendom is to be re-enacted in our present time its outcome may result in somewhat different formulations from those of the past, but scarcely in a substantive change of the affirmation that God is One and that however the doctrine of the *Personae* is stated it must still be affirmed that the Father is not the Son and the Son is not the Father and the Spirit cannot be equated with either. Yet in many churchly pronouncements the faith of Christians is stated as if their one God were Jesus Christ; as if Christ's ministry of reconciliation to the Creator were of no importance; as if the Spirit proceeded only from the Son; as if the Christian Scriptures contained only the New Testament; as if the Old Testament were relevant only insofar as it contained prophecies pointing to Jesus Christ; as if Jesus Christ alone were man's only hope. When this is done the faith of Christians is converted into a Christian religion for which Jesus Christ in isolation is the one object of devotion and in which his own testimony, his very character, his Sonship, his relation to the One with whom he is united, are denied.

This kind of Christian religion has many forms. It is present in popular forms that are similar to Eastern Bhakti and Amida Buddha faiths. It is present in a liberal cult of Jesus and of "the Jesus way of life"; present also in mystical forms as the cultivation of personal companionship with the divine Christ. Historically and theologically we are dealing here with devout yet aberrant forms of faith that are unable to illuminate the more profound problems of human existence, suffering, guilt and destiny or to answer questions about human history in its wholeness. They tend moreover to make of that faith a religion much like all other human religions instead of a relation to the Transcendent that goes beyond all our religions. This confusion of the proximate with the final introduces many internal conflicts into the work of the churches and of theological education. It leads directly to the effort to emphasize the uniqueness of the Christian religion, to define it as the "true" religion, to recommend it because of its originality, to exaggerate the differences between Christian and Jewish faith, to re-erect walls of division that Jesus Christ broke down, to exalt the followers of the one who humbled himself, to define the neighbor as fellow Christian. That the confusion has not led to greater spiritual disasters than have been encountered is doubtless due to the fact that Jesus Christ in his nature and witness is a constant corrective of the perversion of his worship.

Denominationalism not the denominations; ecclesiasticism not the churches; Biblicism not the Bible; Christism not Jesus Christ; these represent the chief present perversions and confusions in Church and theology. There are many other less deceptive, cruder substitutions of the proximate for the ultimate. But the ones described seem to set the great problems to faith and theology in our time. In them the need for a constant process of a radically monotheistic reformation comes to appearance.

If many theological schools today seem uncertain about the context in which they are working and about the purposes they serve this may be due in no small part to the confusions present in that contemporary Christianity itself in which they participate. These internal conflicts are doubtless rooted in the perennial human condition; there is no way to eliminate by any single movement of reformation the temptations and the failures from which the last rebirth alone can set us free. But unless the forms in which idolatries appear at any particular time are illuminated and criticized there is no prospect for ultimate health. The critique of education requires the critique of theology and the critique of theology involves the critique of the Church. Such self-criticism in seminary and Church is always part of that total repentance which is the counterpart of faith.

CHAPTER 2

The Emerging New Conception of the Ministry

I. THE PERPLEXED PROFESSION

A school, we have noted, is related in a double way to the society in which it carries on its work. Participating in the common life it devotes itself to the social objectives in the special way these can be served by a company of scholars or learners who exercise intellectual love of the values toward which the society is directed. In the second place, as one community agency among many, the school also serves the ultimate social objectives indirectly, insofar as its immediate concern is to teach men who will be able to guide and carry on the activities of other agencies; so it functions as a community of teachers. A medical school, for instance, is a research and often also a healing center, directly concerned with the increase of knowledge about the human organism and with its health; but it is also a training center where men are prepared to work in many other institutions of the society, from private practice to public health offices. So also a university in a free society is devoted in intellectual freedom to the pursuit of the universal, liberating knowledge and wisdom that are objectives of the society; it is on the other hand a teaching institution where men are equipped to direct the affairs of the governmental, legal, cultural, educational and economic institutions of the society.

The Protestant schools of theology in the United States and Canada along with all other schools are subject to the tensions inescapably given with this duality of academic functions. But on the whole they are less bothered by them than they might be, for in their relation to the churches they have chosen or been required to devote themselves primarily to the second, that is, to the teaching function of schools. Their express purpose is to educate men who will direct the affairs of church institutions, especially local churches. They tend in consequence to neglect the first function of a theological school—the exercise of the intellectual love of God and neighbor. To this imbalance we shall need to address ourselves in other connections. For the present we must only point out that whatever just criticism may have been made of theological schools in other countries and times because they were too remote from parish and national church activities and because they overlooked their responsibility for training preachers, pastors, evangelists and priests, the North American schools with which we are concerned have not erred in this direction.[1] Their concentration on the task of educating ministers gives them their unique character; it determines the content of their courses of study

[1] Theological schools are characteristically defined in previous reports as institutions for the training of ministers. So William Adams Brown and Mark A. May in *The Education of American Ministers* (New York, 1934), I, 74; III, 3. See also Robert L. Kelly, *Theological Education in America* (New York, 1924), pp. vi, vii–ix, 23–28. The idea of a theological school the present study presupposes is described more fully in Chap. III.

and influences decisively their choice of students, teachers and administrators. It also involves them in great difficulties, since the contemporary Church is confused about the nature of the ministry. Neither ministers nor the schools that nurture them are guided today by a clear-cut, generally accepted conception of the office of the ministry, though such an idea may be emerging.

Similar confusion seems to have characterized some other periods of the Church's history but we shall derive more help toward understanding our situation and its possibilities if we attend to those times when a definite conception of the ministry gave to both those who filled the office and those who prepared them for it a standard by which to judge their work. Such a well-defined idea seems to have prevailed in the Middle Ages. The *Pastoral Rule* of Gregory the Great formulated and disseminated the medieval theory of the minister as the pastoral ruler or the ruling pastor. The pattern was not imposed on the churches by external authority; it grew out of tradition, practice, experience and the needs of the time. Similarly the conception of the minister as priest, though supported by the formidable institutional authority of the Roman Church and its Council of Trent was not legislated into being. The law formulated and gave precision to a conception or a standard that had developed out of traditional and Biblical origins under the influence of historic experiences, resolutions and needs. The theory of the ministry in the churches of the Reformation was also precise; the minister was fundamentally the preacher of the Word, an idea which later, in the days of Pietism and Evangelicalism, was modified in the direction of the conception of the minister as evangelist. In all these instances the men who exercised the

ministry, those to whom they ministered and those who prepared them for their task knew with relative precision what was
expected of the man who held this office.

The confusion about the conception of the ministry characteristic of the time from which we seem to be slowly emerging
was pointed out twenty years ago by Professor Mark A. May.
The conclusion of his study of *The Profession of the Ministry:
Its Status and Problems*[2] was that this confusion presented
theological education with its chief problems. On the one hand,
he pointed out, the very definite concepts of the ministry held
in some quarters conflicted with the desires or needs of students
and congregations and with the temper of the times. On the
other hand, and partly because of such conflict, the idea of the
ministry was vague and uncertain.

What is the function of the minister in the modern community?
The answer is that it is undefined. There is no agreement among
denominational authorities, local officials, seminaries, professors,
prominent laymen, ministers or educators as to what it is or should
be. This lack of agreement, even along the most general lines, is a
characteristic feature of the situation today and accounts in a large
measure for the low educational status of the ministry. The work of
the lawyer, the physician, the teacher, the artist, the writer and the
engineer, is clear-cut and rather sharply defined (at least in the mind
of the average man), so that when a young man chooses one of these
professions he has some idea of what he is getting into. But not so
with the ministry. Entering the ministry is more like entering the
army, where one never knows where he will land or live or what
specific work he will be called upon to perform. This lack of clear
definition of the functions of the pastor that can be widely accepted
influences theological education. . . . How can the seminaries train

[2] May, *The Education of American Ministers*, II, 385–94.

men for a work that is so tenuous, and concerning the nature of which such a diversity of opinion exists?

Much has happened in Church and world, among ministers and laymen, in the years that have elapsed since this judgment was made, and what has happened has led in directions that could not then be foreseen. We can speak today of an emerging new conception of the ministry. But emergence is not yet appearance and in large areas the indefiniteness, vagueness and conflict characteristic of thought about the ministry in the 1930's continues to prevail.

A decade after Professor May's observations had been made Professors Hartshorne and Froyd undertook to study the ministry of the Northern (now American) Baptist Convention. Making their approach from the functional point of view they tried to discover how ministers defined their more important objectives, how they rated the relative importance of their various tasks and how they divided their time in the performance of their duties. The findings of this study indicated how great was the confusion in 1944 even in a single denominational group. It was noted that in the case of a considerable group of ministers "the more conventional patterns are being broken up as these men face the actual needs of their people in the light of increasing knowledge of what these needs are"; that for many others the ministry tends "to drop to the level of a trade, each man being sent into a church with a set of routine procedures, which he is supposed to use indiscriminately in all situations," unequipped, however, with a set of principles such as are necessary for the exercise of a profession.[3]

[3] Huge Hartshorne and Milton C. Froyd, *Theological Education in the Northern Baptist Convention: A Survey* (Philadelphia, 1945), pp. 42, 119.

The evidence that perplexity and vagueness continue to afflict thought about the ministry is to be found today in the theological schools and among ministers themselves. Some schools and some pastors are highly conscious of the problem; others are in a more difficult state because they have not realized the source of their perplexities. In the schools the lack of a clear-cut conception is evident there where a frankly pluralistic approach to the work of the ministry has been accepted and where men are prepared for the varieties of the ministry as well as the varieties of ministerial work without reference to a common function to be carried out by all ministers and by every minister in all the things he does. In these places the course of study consists of a series of preparations for a series of loosely connected acts. In this situation each one of the more general disciplines—such as study of the Bible, theology, church history, psychology, sociology—may then be directly related to a specific function such as preaching, educating, counseling, social action. In the same and in other schools uncertainty about the meaning of the ministry comes to appearance also in the feeling of conflict in a faculty between its loyalty to a traditional idea, such as that of the preacher, and its sense of obligation to denominational officials, alumni and churchmen in general who urge a more "practical" education. Such faculties feel that they are being deflected from their proper work by outside pressures, that they are compromising their ideals and making concessions to expediency when they yield to these demands. Again uncertainty about the meaning of the ministry may be indicated by the silence of many faculties when they are asked to speak of their precise objectives, or by the great generality of the phrases employed when they answer.

Ministers no less than the schools give evidence of the prevailing mistiness of the conception of the ministry. Those who have fought their way through to a clear-cut definition of their task and office often say that they have have had to do this in isolation, without real help from school or Church, and that the maintenance of their sense of specific vocation is a highly personal responsibility. Such men will also point out that the overbusyness of some of their colleagues and the great sense of pressure under which these men work may be due to failure to define what is important and unimportant in a minister's work. The minister who knows what he is doing, they say, is able to resist the many pressures to which he is subject from lay groups in the churches, from the society, from denominational headquarters, and from within himself, however hard he must fight to keep his ship on its course; but the man who has no such determinative principle falls victim to the forces of all the winds and waves that strike upon him. There may be a connection also between indefiniteness in the sense of vocation and the fact that sloth or "downright laziness" is often mentioned by ministers as a reason for failure in the ministry. Doubtless a significant temptation to sloth or "accidie"—as this vice was called in older days—is to be found in the frustration a man experiences when he has no clear sense of his duties and no specific standard by means of which to judge himself. One must not, of course, ascribe too much responsibility to the vagueness of theory. At all times human frailty and sin make the ministry whose business it is to point to the highest reality and the profoundest faith a morally perilous vocation. That "we have this treasure in earthen vessels" is generally very clear to ministers, Church and world. Special temptations abound

for men in this calling—temptations to authoritarianism, to pre-
tentiousness, to self-deception, to love of prestige, to the cultivation of popularity and visible success, et cetera. No matter
how definite the theory of the ministry, the individual pastor
and the whole profession will never be able to drop their guard
against these and more common human temptations to faith-
lessness. Yet when the Church's and the minister's idea about
his work is uncertain it is not unlikely that some of "our calling's
snares" are more than usually difficult to understand and avoid.

Many reasons have been given for the prevalence of this uncertainty and many remedies have been suggested. Some men
believe that it is due to a loss of Christian conviction on the
part of young men and women entering the schools and apply-
ing for ordination or to the weakness of their sense of call to the
ministry. Others, who also see the situation only as a result of
human failure, believe that ministers and schools have been
deflected from their purpose and have lost their sense of mission
because they have succumbed to the temptation to improve
their personal and professional status by doing anything that
might make them pleasing to the greatest number of people.
The voluntaristic system of the free churches in North America,
it has been said, has tended to transform their officials into
merchants who offer all sorts of wares so that as many customers
as possible may be attracted to their ecclesiastical emporiums.
Those who approach the subject sociologically have sometimes
maintained that the difficulty arises out of the fact that many
functions the ministry once discharged have been taken over
by new agencies.

If then, the educational functions of the church have been taken
over by the state, the charity functions by local agencies, so that

pastors now regard the educational and civic among the least important of their activities; and if the number of mid-week prayer services, evangelistic meetings and Sunday evening meetings are declining: if more marriages are being performed by justices of the peace and civil authorities; if attendance at the Sunday morning service is declining owing to golf, radio, good roads, etc.: then what is left for the pastor to do?[4]

So Professor May wrote twenty years ago and his ideas are occasionally echoed in our day, especially in circles that have not participated in or observed the renewal of the Church. It is also pointed out that uncertainty about the office of the ministry may be a by-product of that more intimate interaction among denominations and communions which has been characteristic of recent times. Various ideas are merging: the idea of the preacher as this was worked out in the churches of the Reformation, of the evangelist as this developed in the churches founded during the Revivals, of the priest as represented by the Anglican Catholic movement but also as it becomes effective on Protestants in their relations to the Roman Catholic Church. Yet they are not meeting in such a way as to give rise to a definite new conception but only so as to obscure the definite outlines of each traditional idea. Another sociological explanation of the phenomenon is that the traditional functions of the clergy are not adjusted to the needs of the modern world and that the responsibility for the prevailing uncertainty must be placed on the Church as a cultural laggard which has not kept up with the times.

There seems to be a measure of truth in each of these statements. Temptations to abandon the proper work of the ministry

[4] May, *Education of American Ministers*, II. 389.

because of ambition or the desire to please are encountered—
and succumbed to—at all times. Temptations to continue a
traditional course by virtue of sheer inertia are also familiarly
human. But what critics who point to these reasons for the
loss of certainty seem too often to forget is that the Church is
never only a function of a culture nor ever only a supercultural
community; that the problem of its ministers is always how to
remain faithful servants of the Church in the midst of cultural
change and yet to change culturally so as to be true to the
Church's purpose in new situations. Those who suggest that
the ministry should provide for its continuation by turning itself into a kind of social or counseling service ignore the nature
of the ministry and really provide for its discontinuation. So do
those who seek a remedy for present ills by insisting on un-
changing adherence to a form of the ministry developed in some
earlier cultural period.

During the time in which analyses of the sort we have alluded
to were being made and such remedies proposed, and in part
tried, an unspectacular process of reconstruction has been going
on in Church and ministry so that we can speak today of an
emerging new conception of the ministry, a conception which
leaves it ministry and does not change it into something else.
It is a conception which has not been manufactured in the
study, though theologians in their studies have contributed to
its development. It has grown out of the wrestlings of ministers
with their problems, out of the experiences of the times and
the needs of men, yet it has its roots in the Bible and in the long
tradition of the Church. In time it may be so formulated that
schools training men for the ministry will have as clear a picture
before them of their immediate objective as their predecessors

had when the ideas of the pastoral ruler, the priest, the preacher
and the evangelist prevailed. Ministers also and the laity of the
Church will know what is expected of those who hold this
office. For the present it is possible only to feel after and to
describe in sketchy outline what this new conception is, a conception that we may believe is at least as much gift of grace
as consequence of sin and perhaps more something produced
by historic forces under divine government than the creature
of human pride and fickleness. Before we undertake to set
forth our understanding of this emerging new idea we need to
analyze what the elements are that constitute any such pattern.

II. PASTORS, PREACHERS AND PRIESTS

Whenever in Christian history there has been a definite, intelligible conception of the ministry four things at least were
known about the office: what its chief work was and what the
chief purpose of all its functions; what constituted a call to the
ministry; what was the source of the minister's authority; and
whom the minister served.

a. *The Work of the Ministry.* Since the days described in the
New Testament Christian ministers have preached and taught;
they have led worship and administered sacraments; they have
presided over the church and exercised oversight over its work;
they have given pastoral care to individuals in need. Though at
times these functions have been distributed among specialized
orders of the clergy, still each minister, in his own domain, has
needed to exercise all of them. Yet whenever there has been a
clear conception of the office one of these functions has been
regarded as central and the other functions have been ordered
so as to serve, not indeed it, but, the chief purpose that it

served directly. In the case of the medieval pastoral ruler of Gregory's description it seems evident that the chief ministerial function was the exercise of that "art of arts," the government of souls. The pastoral ruler also preached; he also administered the sacraments and led the service of worship; he also supervised the activities of the church; but all these other indispensable activities were directed toward the same end as the care and government of souls. Preaching and sacrament and church administration were dominated by the purpose of so directing needy souls that they might escape from the snares of sin and achieve everlasting life. The great motive was love of neighbor and this was found to be in a certain tension with the love of God, since the latter prompted a servant of the Lord to shun worldly duties as well as distractions and to give his life to adoration and contemplation in monastic seclusion. The great purpose of saving souls from hell was most directly served through the penitential office, but it was also to be achieved through preaching, teaching, prayer and church administration.

Similarly the preacher of the churches of the Reformation carried on all the traditional functions of the ministry. He preached and taught; he administered the sacraments and led in prayer; he presided over the church and he cared for the needy. Yet there was no question about his chief office nor about the chief purpose which he had before him in the performance of all traditional or new functions. His main work was preaching the gospel of forgiveness, declaring God's love for man as revealed in Jesus Christ. And in all his other work the objective of such preaching was the guiding purpose. The objective was salvation. Salvation meant for him as for the pastoral ruler deliverance from the pains of hell, yet not quite so much this as forgiveness of sin and reconciliation with God with all their consequences. The purpose of the ministry was the renewal of life by evangelical faith in God's love for man. As the minister's first work was always the preaching of the gospel of divine love, so all his other activities were directed to the same proximate end of bringing men to a personal, internal apprehension of the good news, an apprehension which resulted in genuine repentance and trust. The meaning of worship and of the administration of the sacraments lay in their preparation for, or their response to, the gospel. The care of souls was a matter of personal admonition and consolation addressed to men who needed to apprehend in penitence and confidence the forgiveness of sin, the great love of God extended toward them, so that in life and death, in sin and sorrow, they knew they were in the hands of a holy, loving God. Churches were organized and administered with this purpose in view. The church building was designed as a place where the gospel could be preached; the laity was organized to support the preaching; the instruction of youth was in catechisms that set forth the content of the gospel. The minister might be tempted, as Richard Baxter's *The Reformed Pastor* points out, to conceive his office too narrowly as consisting only of public preaching. But even for Baxter preaching was the most excellent part of the pastor's work. Moreover, for the ministers of the Reformed churches "preaching" was a symbolic word; it meant not only public discourse but every action through which the gospel was brought home and men were moved to repent before God and to trust in him. Public discourse was never enough; private admonition, catechetical instruction, personal pastoral care, the administra tion of the sacrament, the leadership of public worship—all these needed to be faithfully attended to; but in everything he did the preacher had one thing to do, namely, to bring home to men the gospel of divine love.

The evangelist of the Wesleyan, Evangelical, Pietist movement represented a variation on the Protestant idea of the preacher. Even more than the minister of the Reformation churches he found his chief function in preaching; insofar as he was often a traveling evangelist he discharged the other traditional functions of the ministry less frequently than the Reformed or Lutheran pastor. So long, however, as he was only evangelist he needed to consider himself as belonging to only one of several orders of ministers, an order which like that of the preaching friars of the thirteenth century required the accompanying work of the "secular clergy" or of the local parsons. When he became the settled minister of a local church he needed to add to the preaching function the other activities of the ministry—the care of souls, the administration of the sacraments, the conduct of public worship, the government of the church. But the organizing principle of all these activities was the evangelical conversion and sanctification of souls, which was the direct purpose of the evangelistic sermon.

The distinction of the priest-minister from the preacher-minister is relatively easy to make. Though both perform the same functions these are organized in different ways both in relation to each other and to a central purpose. From Chrysostom ("On the Priesthood") to Pius XI ("On the Catholic Priesthood") the idea of the priesthood is marked by emphasis on the importance and greatness of the work of administering the sacraments. The priest also teaches and preaches; he governs and

cures souls; he presides over the church; but above all he offers
the sacrifice of Christ in the Eucharist and is the minister of
those sacraments "through which the grace of the Savior flows
for the good of mankind." The purpose of the sacraments is
the reconciliation of God and man, a reconciliation of God to
man as well as of man to God, for the priest is always the
mediator between God and humanity. This reconciliation is
the precondition for the exercise not only of man's love to God
and neighbor but also of God's love to man. It is the proximate
purpose of the chief sacramental act but also of every other
exercise of the priestly office. Few exponents of the priestly
idea want to confine priestly activity to the administration of
the central sacrament, just as few Reformers understand the
preaching minister as solely a preacher. The priest exercises
"the ministry of the word," says Pope Pius XI, describing in
some detail what this ministry is; the priest, furthermore, leads
in public and official prayer, in intercession, adoration and
thanksgiving; he is the "tireless furtherer of the Christian education of youth," defends the sanctity of marriage, contributes to
the solution of social conflicts, and is the "most valorous leader"
in the crusade of "expiation and penance." But in all his acts
he serves the purpose chiefly served in the administration of
the sacrament—the purpose of mediating between God and
man.

As these examples of typical ideas of the ministry all indicate,
a clear-cut conception always includes not only an understanding of what the most important work of the ministry is but also
the recognition that it must perform other functions. Unity is
given to such a conception not only by ordering functions in a
scale of importance but by directing each function to a chief,

though still proximate, end. Now that end is the salvation of souls from eternal punishment, now the cure of guilty souls through their apprehension of the love of God, now the reconciliation of God and man through sacrifice and sacrament and works of expiation. If there is confusion in the conception of the ministry today, whether only among those who once held to the ideal of the preacher or also among those who have maintained the ideal of the priest, that confusion appears at both points—in inability to define what the most important activity of the ministry is and in uncertainty about the proximate end toward which all its activities are directed. If a new conception of the ministry is emerging it will be marked by the appearance of a sense of the relative importance of the activities and a definite idea of the proximate end sought by the minister in all of them.

b. *The Call to the Ministry.* A definite understanding of the ministerial office also includes a relatively clear-cut conception of what constitutes the call to the ministry. How and by whom are men appointed to this office? Once more, differences in historic definitions of the ministry are less due to exclusive insistence on some one interpretation of what constitutes a call than to variations in the emphasis placed on the various elements present in every call. Christians of all ages and churches have encountered in their reading of Scriptures socially appointed, institutionally recognized priests, prophets and apostles, but also extraordinary, "natural" or "charismatic" leaders—non-Levitical priests, prophets without human appointment and apostles chosen like Paul. In their contemporary experience they have dealt with both types of ministers and have found virtues and vices attached to both types. Even the most highly organized churches which insist on the importance of "legitimate" orders recognize with the Church of England that "there always remains the power of God to give to the Church prophets, evangelists and teachers apart from the succession," and even the most spiritualistic groups will elect certain men to interpret the sense of meetings in which anyone moved by the spirit is allowed to speak.

It appears that there is general though only implicit recognition of the fact that a call to the ministry includes at least these four elements: (1) the *call to be a Christian*, which is variously described as the call to discipleship of Jesus Christ, to hearing and doing of the Word of God, to repentance and faith, et cetera; (2) *the secret call*, namely, that inner persuasion or experience whereby a person feels himself directly summoned or invited by God to take up the work of the ministry; (3) *the providential call*, which is that invitation and command to assume the work of the ministry which comes through the equipment of a person with the talents necessary for the exercise of the office and through the divine guidance of his life by all its circumstances; (4) *the ecclesiastical call*, that is, the summons and invitation extended to a man by some community or institution of the Church to engage in the work of the ministry. At no time have the Church and the churches not required of candidates for the ministry that they be first of all men of Christian conviction, however such conviction and its guarantees were interpreted. The Church everywhere and always has expected its ministers to have a personal sense of vocation, forged in the solitariness of encounter with ultimate claims made upon them. It has also generally required that they show evidence of the fact that they have been chosen for the task by the divine bestowal upon them, through birth and experience, of the intellectual, moral, physical and psychological gifts necessary for the work of the ministry. Finally, in one form or another, it has required that they be summoned or invited or at least accepted by that part of the Church in which they undertake to serve. But ideas of the ministry have varied as Christian call, secret call, providential call and church call have been related to one another in varying orders of importance and modes of relationship. In the cases of the pastoral ruler of Gregory the Great and of Chrysostom's priest the summons of the church to men whom it found divinely chosen by Christian and providential call was of the first importance. The secret call, the summons and decision that occurred in solitariness, usually came after the public or church call. In the case of the evangelist, however, the order of these calls was reversed. "I allow," said John Wesley, "that it is highly expedient, whoever preaches in his name should have an outward as well as inward call; but that it is *absolutely necessary* I deny." More extremely, early Friends not only maintained that the "inward call, or testimony of the Spirit" was "essential and necessary to a minister" but denied the validity of the church call and seemed indifferent to the providential call, at least insofar as they discounted the significance of "birth-right" Christianity. Whatever the variations, it seems true that when a clear idea of the ministry prevailed there was also a clear idea of what constituted a call to the ministry and for the most part such a clear idea took into account the necessity of all four calls and ordered their relations.

Modern vagueness in thought about the ministry appears in the uncertainty of the churches, the ministers themselves, of boards and schools about the nature of the call. This vagueness doubtless is partly due to the conflict of traditions—a conflict in which exponents of the primacy of the "secret call" may take the position that it alone is adequate while others who emphasize the first importance of church call come to the indefensible position of renouncing the importance of command and obedience enacted in solitariness. It may be due also to the inapplicability to the Christian experience of young persons in our time of a theory of call developed in another age of Christian experience—the age of revivalism and evangelicalism. Whatever the reasons for the uncertainty, there is evidence that a new idea of call is emerging among Protestant churches and is contributing its share to the emerging new concept of the ministry. The idea is not a simple one but an idea of order and relation in the complex action and interaction of person, community and God, governing providentially, working by his spirit, active in history. But the further description of this idea of the call must be deferred for a moment while we undertake to analyze other elements that enter into the definition of the ministry.

c. *The Minister's Authority.* In those periods when clear-cut ideas of the ministry prevailed pastors and people were relatively agreed on the acceptable answer to the question: By what authority do you do these things, i.e., preach, care for souls, preside over the church and administer the sacraments? Today, however, answers to the question are frequently uncertain and vague.

Authority, to be sure, is a complex phenomenon and some elements in the power which office-bearers exercise at any given time and place as well as in the respect accorded to them cannot easily be stated in conceptual terms. An effort to analyze the authority of the ministry as this was exercised and recognized in the early and medieval Church and in the centuries immediately after the Reformation would lead us deep into social history and psychology, into theology and political science. The further effort to account for the loss of pastoral authority in the modern world would require no less extensive researches into the effects on men of the democratic, industrial, technological and scientific revolutions. Such detailed inquiries lie beyond the scope of this study; we must content ourselves with a few reflections on the various answers to the question about ministerial authority that have been given at different times.

In those answers there has always been indirect reference to the ultimate power that lies behind all human authority, but the defined source of authority has been some mediate principle. Only in the case of the prophet or some other exceptionable person has the answer pointed more directly to God as the giver of the authority. The ministry in general and the Church, as community and as institution, have been highly aware that false prophets claiming immediate empowerment by the Divine always greatly exceed in number the true spokesmen for God, that there are more lying visions than authentic ones, and that personal inspirations must be subjected to social or historical validation. Hence though the minister in all times is "man of God" he does not as minister undertake to prophesy with a "Thus says the Lord," and to claim that his words are the Word of God. He is "man of God" at least in the sense that his office is as such a human acknowledgment of the sovereignty of God, as the Church in its very existence is a confession of faith in God. But the authority which accrues to him as such an official witness to divine authority is neither under his nor the Church's control. In times of great unbelief his social authority will be diminished by the fact that the office points to divine authority; he will participate in the humiliation rather than in the exaltation of Christ. While then the office of the ministry refers to ultimate authority the reference is more by way of indication than of representation. Even prophecy points to divine power more than it regards itself as the vehicle of that power; and the ambassador for Christ is no plenipotentiary. Hence when we ask about the authority of the ministry we leave aside, though we do not forget, his authority as "man of God" and "ambassador for Christ."

We must also leave aside, and in this case try to forget, several sorts of incidental authority that have accrued to ministers at various times because of the interactions of Church and world. Among these is the authority of government which is attached to the ministry when Church and state are so closely united that the minister is also an official of the state and represents it in the discharge of his functions. Something of this ambivalent authority remains even when Church and state are separated, as in the case of the military chaplaincy and in the authorization of ministers by governments to perform civilly sanctioned marriage rites. Again the authority of the minister as representative of the community of learning is incidental and not essential to the office. That he ought to be well educated is one thing, but that he ought to have the authority of learning is something else. For a long time in Western history clergymen, like the priests of ancient Egypt, were the only learned group and hence represented the mystery and power of learning. Now it is often bewailed that they have lost that authority and it may be maintained that the fault is theirs or the Church's for not insisting sufficiently on an educated ministry. But the loss of this authority seems due far more to the rise of a large and varied group of learned men in many other professions than to a failure on the part of the Church and ministry as such to maintain previously established standards. The loss of social power by the ministry as a result of the spread of education and the transference to scientists of the representative authority of learning is comparable to the loss ministers suffered when Church and state were separated. Neither civil power nor learning in itself form the basis of ministerial authority however much they may contribute at certain times to the prestige of the ministry.

Ministers have derived their immediate authority to preach and teach, lead worship, care for souls and perform their other offices from the Church and from Scripture. When they have been asked about their authority they have pointed to these two "powers" as the ones they represent. Accordingly they have been questioned about the extent to which they truly represented them and have been accorded the kind of respect which was extended at the time to Church and Scriptures. But within this framework of validation by Church and Scriptures there have been many variations in the ministers' and the churches' conceptions of pastoral authority. For one thing there have been differences in the order of precedence as between Church and Scriptures. For another, there has been variation insofar as now Church as institution, now Church as community has been the source of authority. And again changes have occurred as in some instances the delegation, in others the acquisition, of power has been emphasized.

Ministers at all times have exercised authority as representatives of churchly institutions and the dignity of the institutional

Church, the respect accorded to it—whatever its measure at the time—have been in some ways transferred to them. They have also been spokesmen of the Church as community, have represented the mind and tradition of the Church, and so they have exercised the kind of communal authority that accrues to the person who represents the community to itself; for instance, in the parallel case of a national community a leader such as Abraham Lincoln, quite apart from his institutional authority as president representing the state, has particular power as the exponent of the national mind and spirit. Ministers have been, further, representatives of the Scriptures, as interpreters possessing the authority of teachers, and often as judges charged with the responsibility of deciding definitively, though not infallibly, what the meaning of the Church's constitution is in a particular situation.

Finally, it has been expected of ministers that they should acquire the authority possessed by those who have directly experienced what they commend to others. This also is a kind of teaching authority, but even more the authority of the witness. As preachers of the gospel it is expected that they themselves have experienced its power; as guides to the life of penitence and faith they need to know directly the nature of the humble and contrite heart. They cannot teach the law without being under the law nor unlovingly seek to increase love; when they attempt to do so their work lacks authority. Though the authority of experience and character is gift of grace it is also achievement on the part of men who work out their salvation with fear and trembling because God works in them.

These various kinds of authority—church authority as institutional and communal, Scriptural authority as teaching and judicatory, personal authority as spiritual and moral—are intricately interrelated. In some conceptions of the ministry one or the other sort may be entirely lacking, or, as in the case of judicatory authority, may be transferred by communal or institutional decision to certain ministers or companies of them or to representative bodies of clergy and laity. Nevertheless, when we ask the pastoral ruler or the priest or the preacher and evangelist by what authority he carries on his work his answer usually seems to include reference to all these sources of his empowerment. But there are striking differences in the order in which they are mentioned.

The authority of the priest is first of all institutional. His ordination is mentioned first, then his personal discipline of life, and his study of the Scriptures and the mind of the community. His "august powers," says Pope Pius XI, "are conferred upon the priest in a special Sacrament designed to this end." These powers include "power over the very body of Jesus Christ" to make "it present upon our altars" and "the power which . . . 'God gave neither to Angels nor Archangels'—the power to remit sins." The priest, however, must exercise other functions besides administering the sacraments and institutional means cannot empower him to fulfill these duties; hence he needs to practice spiritual discipline, cultivating all the Christian virtues; he also needs to study, for "how can he teach unless he himself possess knowledge" and have gained a "full grasp of the Catholic teaching on faith and morals?"

The sources of the authority of the pastoral ruler Gregory the Great describes are doubtless the same, but as his functions are differently ordered from those of the modern priest so also the bases of his power are mentioned in a different order and with a varying emphasis. The primary source of his authority seems to lie in the personal discipline that enables him, as one who knows how to govern himself as Christian, also to govern and guide others. Ordination can be taken for granted but it seems clear that ordination cannot give the pastoral ruler the strength he requires. Personal experience and discipline as well as study of the Scriptures are the foundation stones of his authority.

The preacher of the Reformation needs institutional empowerment, but ordination plays no such role in his accreditation as do first of all the study and personal appropriation of Scriptures and especially of the gospel, and, secondly, the corresponding discipline of life. In the case of the evangelist institutional ordination can become a matter of wholly minor significance and even the study of Scriptures is often made secondary to personal experience of the power of the gospel. To the priest, the pastoral ruler, the preacher and the evangelist we may add the churchman, the kind of minister, appearing in many periods, who exercises authority in the interpretation of the Scriptures, in the direction of the church, in the leadership of prayer and the care of souls as one who participates deeply in the mind of the community and who has acquired communal authority by study and discipline. Such men—Bernard of Clairvaux is one representative of the type—will also be institutionally authorized, but their authority comes from the community more than from the institution, and their relation to the Scriptures is that of members of the interpreting and obeying community rather than that of isolated individuals.

The confusion in modern Christendom about the meaning of the ministry makes itself evident in uncertainty about pastoral authority as well as in the vagueness present in thought about pastoral functions. Outside the Roman Catholic Church institutional authority is generally weak, partly because in their pluralism the institutions too clearly represent something else than God, Christ and Scriptures or the Christian community. These local churches and denominations, greatly loved as they are by their members, are not so hedged by divinity that pronouncements made in their name invite reverent attention. The ambiguous, sometimes slightly amused attitude many laymen betray toward ordination may be somewhat indicative of the lack of power in the institutional aspect of the ministry. The power of the Scriptures remains very great but that power is ill-defined today when the older theories about the nature of Scriptural authority have been eroded and the Christian's present understanding of it remains still to be formulated. The minister who is a faithful interpreter of the Word continues to exercise considerable authority because of the actual power of the Bible, but not a few ministers themselves have been uncertain about its authority and have not mediated it since they were not subject to it themselves. Communal authority has been weakened by the individualization of religious life in the fragmented modern world and by loss of continuity with the past. To many men there has remained only the spiritual authority they derived from personal religious life, or, as a spurious substitute for any kind of authority, personal attractiveness whether genuine or fictitious. One may speak of a general weakening of the authority of the ministry in the modern world. This weakening may be the ecclesiastical counterpart of that decline of respect for authority which has occurred among men who first having thought themselves masters of their fate then, as mass-men, became the prey of powers which moved them about not as persons but as things or bundles of conditionable reflexes. To such men no power was anything but brute force, unentitled to respect; every word was simple propaganda.

Since this problem of authority among men is always ultimately theological the crisis in pastoral authority is symptomatic of the crisis in civilization, though it is not as some apologists for the Church seem to believe the cause of the latter crisis. At all events it seems true that with increase among men of respect for the Church and Scriptures, above all with increased awareness of the sovereignty of God, the authority of the pastor who represents or at least points to these powers also increases. But the problem remains how and what he is to represent in the first place and how such representation can come about.

d. *The Idea of the People.* The final element in a theory of the ministry which we can consider here is the notion of the people to whom the ministers are sent as servants. When the idea of the ministry is relatively well-defined both of these questions are answered: Is the minister primarily sent to the people of the Church or to those of the world? What, in the light of Christian faith, is the greatest need of the people to whom he is sent, that one need which amidst all their needs is always to be kept in view by the minister?

The relations of Church and world being what they are no ministry has ever been exclusively directed to those within or to those outside the Christian community. Even when the minister begins as missionary to some people in the world he soon gathers a Church that claims his special attention; even when he begins as a shepherd of a separated flock he is bound to have relations to those who seem to be the wolves that prey upon it or the dogs that protect it. Still, there are differences of emphasis. When the Church is regarded as all-inclusive and locally becomes the parish Church, universally the ecumenical Church, then the ministry knows itself to be the servant of all it can reach since all are nominally in the Church. When the Church is regarded as exclusive, separated from the rest of society, an ark of salvation in a great flood of destruction, then the emphasis falls on service to the elect few. Today there is uncertainty about the ministry in Church and world partly because it is not clear whether the Church is fundamentally inclusive or exclusive, whether therefore the minister's concern is to extend to all in his reach or only to a faithful elite. Is the rural, the suburban, the inner-city, the college minister a parish parson or a builder of a separated community? Is the theological teacher a minister of a separate, ecclesiastical science or of a university subject?

A definite theory of the ministry always includes, furthermore, specific awareness of the nature and fundamental need of the people it serves. When Gregory wrote his *Pastoral Rule* there was present to his mind the immature and sinful yet immortal race whose members needed the service of the pastoral ruler on their wayward course of life that they might escape hell and enter into heaven's joy. The understanding of man characteristic of the Reformers was that of a sublime but perverted creation, a ruined work of art, Milton's Adam. He was a highly dynamic, willful, loving and rebellious being, whose power was thwarted, whose will was in bondage, whose love and anger were misdirected. His fundamental need was for reconciliation to God through repentance and faith. All other

wants were secondary to the need for the experienced forgiveness of his sin. Gregory as well as Luther and Calvin knew that
man lacked many other things besides the one thing needful
and that the cure of all his other diseases would not ensue
automatically on the healing of his deepest wound. But they
knew where to begin their ministry, to what human need ministers as ministers needed to address themselves in all their
words and deeds, whatever else they might be required to do
because physicians, social workers, teachers and lawyers were
not available.

For a long time now the Christian understanding of man
has been obscured by theories of his nature built on other dogmas than that of the sovereignty of God and constructed out of
observations of his behavior made from other points of view
than those of Christian faith. As the conception of nature to
which man is always related has changed, churches and ministers have often succumbed to the temptation to substitute
the needs of natural man (that is, of man as primarily related
to nature) for the needs of theological man (that is, of man as
primarily related to God). Or again, as the great significance of
the individual's relation to society became clear the needs of
social man seemed to be primary. But the traditional work of
the ministry in teaching the Word from God, the word to God
and words about God, of administering the sacraments, of
building the Church and caring for souls seemed to have too
little direct relevance to the needs of men so naturalistically
or socially understood. Was not the approach to the needs of
such men from natural or social science more direct and more
helpful than the circuitous approach from divine science?
Hence great discussions developed over the question how to

make the gospel relevant to needs it never had had primarily in view. It was translated into evolutionary and social terms, though it resisted efforts to cast it into such strange forms. Confusion was bound to result. The political needs of men struggling for survival or status, the economic needs of hungry and competitive men, the psychological needs of anxious and guilty interpersonal beings, these and other highly important wants seemed to require the ministrations of the Church. And to justify themselves churches and ministers had before them the example of the Great Physician and Reformer who had compassion on every man in natural need and prophesied to an oppressed, divided nation threatened by disaster. The context in which he did these things, the cause for which he came out and why he was sent was often forgotten.

In this situation some ministers abandoned the ministry for medicine or social service, while others attempted to transform their traditional work into semiclinical or social service activity. The great mass of clergymen remained true to their primary calling but they were puzzled. There was good reason for their perplexity, for the theological view of man is always bound up with natural and social views of man and what had happened was that old views of nature and society had changed radically. How to understand men as fundamentally related to God when their relations to nature and society had so changed presented a most difficult practical as well as theoretical problem. The temptation to try to convert the concept of the ministry from one directed to the needs of man-in-relation-to-God to one directed toward the wants of natural or social man was the more attractive because the alternative seemed to be a ministry that could not speak of God and man in their relations to each other without employing thirteenth- and sixteenth-century conceptions of nature and society. Often the ministry seemed to be divided between those who sought to make the gospel relevant by allegorizing it so as to meet the needs of modern men and those who regarded its earlier translations as so literal that any new translation was betrayal. Most clergymen probably avoided these extremes, but their problems were so much the greater.

The confusion is lifting somewhat. Out of the great wrestlings of men with their personal and social problems, out of renewed study of Scriptures and critical reflection on history, a view of man is emerging that sets in the forefront again his relation to God. The scene in which the divine-human encounter takes place is not, to be sure, a flat earth canopied by a heavenly tent; the scene has become stranger and vaster. The human protagonist in this encounter is not a being that thinks with heart and kidneys; he has become an even more mysterious creature. The history of his wrestle with God is not confined to a few thousand years of dramatic events occurring in Asia Minor, though the crucial importance of those events seems even greater as the story expands into remoter pasts and futures. But still, man is seen as man engaged in conflict, conversation and reconciliation with God. Before the new yet old view comes clear an incalculable amount of work must be done by poets and theologians, by historical scholars and Biblical students, by ministers dealing at close range with men in this encounter, and especially by these men themselves. Those among them most conversant with nature and society in their modern aspects must make particular contributions. Nevertheless, as soon as man has been understood as man-before-God confusion about the nature of the ministry has begun to disappear, no matter how great the remaining problems of "demythologizing" and translating the gospel and the law.

III. THE PASTORAL DIRECTOR

In the foregoing analysis of the elements that enter into any well-defined theory of the ministry some indications have been given of the character of that theory which seems to be emerging out of contemporary study of the Bible, participation in the tradition of the Church, the experiences and reflections of ministers in our day, and the needs of the time. Each of these is an important source of the emerging idea and signs of its appearance are to be found in all the centers of church activity—in the theological schools, in the conferences and discussions of churchmen, and, above all, in the work and thought of ministers themselves. The new idea is not equally significant everywhere, for in some areas older conceptions—those of the priest, the preacher and the evangelist—remain more pertinent than the new. Yet the developing idea seems more widely significant and applicable than is often believed by those who are holding fast to the earlier conceptions. Priests are affected by it as well as preachers[5]; rural no less than urban ministers are challenged to develop a ministry in accordance with it; it applies to the ministers whose provinces are denominations or regions as well as to those whose concern is a neighborhood. We cannot here raise the question about the part cultural changes on the one hand, renewed Christian convictions and the new sense of Church on the other, play in its development. Our problem is to describe the theory that seems to be emerging and to be gaining ground

[5] Cf. Joseph H. Fichter, s.j., *Social Relations in the Urban Parish* (Chicago 1954), Chap. X, "Social Roles of the Parish Priest."

in the thought as well as the practice of ministers. For want of a better phrase we may name it the conception of the minister as a pastoral director, though the name is of little importance.

What the term is meant to designate is indicated rather indirectly by the character of modern church architecture and by the perverted form in which the idea occurs. The place in which the minister mainly functions always signalizes the Church's idea of his task. The building and room in which the priest discharges his office is designed for the celebration of the mass; it is dominated by the altar, though provision is also made in it for preaching and confession. The space in which the preacher does his work is a room in which the pulpit with its open Bible is the central feature though provision is also made for the administration of the sacraments and sometimes for meetings of the ruling elders. The period of greatest confusion in Protestant conceptions of Church and ministry was marked by the conversion of the room into a place in which organ, choir, pulpit and communion table simultaneously claimed first attention and Akron-plan Sunday School rooms were extruded from an amoebic nucleus. To be sure, contemporary church architecture continues to betray how uncertain and groping are the efforts of the Church to define the nature of its ministry. Some of it is symptomatic of an experimentation controlled by no leading idea but only by vagary and the desire to please as many potential church visitors as possible. Yet there is a dominant movement so that the modern Protestant church building, not to speak now of the Roman Catholic, becomes a sign of what is being done in it. What is being done is evidently a very complex thing for these many rooms of the parish house or religious education building, are designed for a great number of meetings besides those of Sunday School classes and official boards. But the manifoldness is not unorganized. The focal center of the complex building is a room for which no name yet has been found. To call it either auditorium or sanctuary seems false. It is the place of worship and of instruction. The prominence given to Holy Table or altar, to cross and candles, does not indicate so much that this is the place where the sacraments are celebrated as that it is the place of prayer. The pulpit, however, has not been relegated to a secondary place as though preaching were not now important. Another architectural feature is symptomatic. The minister now has an office from which he directs the activities of the Church, where also he studies and does some of his pastoral counseling.

A second indirect indication of the character of the new conception of the ministry may be gained from a glance at its perverse form—the one in which the pastoral director becomes the "big operator." When ministers comment on the kinds of men who are failures in the ministry they frequently describe among these types the person who operates a religious club or a neighborhood society with much efficiency and pomp and circumstance. He is active in many affairs, organizes many societies, advertises the increases in membership and budget achieved under his administration and, in general, manages church business as if it were akin to the activities of a chamber of commerce. In their reaction to such secularization of the office some men try to return to the idea of the preacher or of the priest. But the needs of men and the responsibilities of office prevent them from doing so. Then they realize that the "big operator" represents a perversion of the minister's office not because he is an executive but because he does not administer the church's work.

The pastoral director of a contemporary church has his historical antecedent. His predecessor is to be found in the bishop or overseer of an ancient church, a man who, unlike modern bishops, was not primarily entrusted with oversight over many clergymen and local churches but was elected to oversee a single local church. As bishop of Hippo Regius Augustine was such a pastoral director. The bishops described in the First Letter to Timothy were such men—the heads and overseers of the Household of God.

In his work the pastoral director carries on all the traditional functions of the ministry—preaching, leading the worshiping community, administering the sacraments, caring for souls, presiding over the church. But as the preacher and priest organized these traditional functions in special ways so does the pastoral director. His first function is that of building or "edifying" the church; he is concerned in everything that he does to bring into being a people of God who as a Church will serve the purpose of the Church in the local community and the world. Preaching does not become less important for him than it was for the preacher but its aim is somewhat different. It is now pastoral preaching directed toward the instruction, the persuasion, the counseling of persons who are becoming members of the body of Christ and who are carrying on the mission of the Church. It is therefore at its best more inclusively Biblical rather than evangelical only; it is directed indeed to sinful men who need to be reconciled to God but also to men who need in all things to grow up into mature manhood in the measure of the stature of the fullness of Christ and who are to interpret to others the meaning of Christian faith. Leading the "royal priesthood" of the whole Church in worship becomes more important for this pastoral director than it had been for the preacher; this worship is not simply the accompaniment of the preaching of the gospel but the effort of the Church to demonstrate its love of God, whose love of man is being proclaimed in the gospel. The activity of the Church as a priesthood making intercession for all men, offering thanks and praise on behalf of all, now requires the minister's devoted leadership in a particular way. The activity on behalf of individuals is for this pastoral director not only a matter of pastoral rule or of the pastoral cure of souls, though it will include both, but is best designated as pastoral counseling, a counseling that has them in view as needing reconciliation to God but also to men, yet knows that reconciliation is not automatically productive of wisdom. It is a counseling, moreover, that calls into service the aid of many other men and agencies able to help a person in need, and, very frequently, it is a counseling of counselors. So also as teacher, the pastoral director becomes the teacher of teachers, the head of all educational organization which he cannot simply manage but must lead as a competent Christian educator. These and other less central activities of the ministry of all periods are carried on by the pastoral director, but the work that lays the greatest claim to his time and thought is the care of a church, the administration of a community that is directed toward the whole purpose of the Church, namely, the increase among men of the love of God and neighbor; for the Church is becoming the minister and its "minister" is its servant, directing it in its service.

It is significant that when ministers reflect on their theological education they are likely to regret more than any other deficiency in it the failure of the school to prepare them for the administration of such a church. What these men have in mind was expressed by one of them who said in effect: The seminary prepared me for preaching and taught me the difference between preaching and public speaking; it helped me to become a *pastoral* counselor and not simply a counselor; it prepared me for the work of *Christian* education; but it gave me no preparation to administer a church as Church; what I learned about church administration was a nontheological smattering of successful business practices. It may also be significant that a superintendent bewailed the fact that while he would like to find for the churches under his care the best preachers available these churches themselves were not so concerned about preaching; they wanted "all-round men."

In the contemporary situation the idea of the minister's call is undergoing a change in the direction of greater emphasis on the significance of the call extended to a person by the Church on the basis of its understanding of his Christian and providential calling. The secret call as always remains important, but in the conception of the ministry that is emerging out of the Biblical and systematic theology of the day and out of the personal reflections of young people and their pastors, the divine action whereby men are chosen for their station and calling is less spiritualistically understood than was the case for the past hundred years. The mode of election whereby God appoints individuals to their lifework is seen as not different in character from the mode whereby he elects them to serve him as men or women, as American or Asian, as first- or twentieth-century men. In every case, to be sure, the call requires internal apprehension of the divine will, the response of human will, the acceptance of the yoke of the kingdom. Without a personal sense of vocation gained in the solitary struggles of the soul with its Maker and Redeemer the minister will always be deficient. But the call to the ministry is not for our contemporaries first of all a mystic matter enacted in the solitariness of lonesome encounter; it is rather a call extended to social man, the member of a community, through the mediation of community. It is more like the call of Stephen than of Paul, of Ambrose and Augustine than of Francis of Assisi, of Calvin than of Fox. Young men and women today feel themselves challenged to identify themselves with the community and institution devoted to the service of God rather than with an ideal; the human need of which they are made aware is one that only the community can minister to; the words through which they hear the Word of God addressed to them are likely to be the words of the Church. As the conception of the work of the ministry changes into the idea of the whole Church ministering so the conception of call changes into the idea of the called and the calling Church—always, of course, as Church under the authority of God. In such a situation the providential call assumes increased importance, for the question the Church raises through its various agencies is which young men and women have been endowed by God with the spiritual, moral and intellectual qualities necessary to this work, which of them through the guidance of their lives have been led by God toward the ministry, which of them it ought therefore to call. Hence also the Church requiring young people to consider whether they are not called of God to this work asks them to reflect especially on the requirements he has laid upon them by his watchful providence over the whole course of their lives and by bringing them into being in this time with its needs.

As in the cases of the ministry's functions and of the call so also when the minister's authority is in question the Church moves nearer the center of the picture in the emerging new conception. The ministry of today and tomorrow must indeed represent all the kinds of authority associated with the office in the past—institutional, teaching or Scriptural, communal and spiritual; but as institutional authority was central in the priest's office and Scriptural in the preacher's so communal authority becomes of greatest importance to the pastoral director. He will continue to be ordained by the institution and will, if he is faithful to it, have as much authority as the institution he represents has; spiritual authority is as necessary to him as to ministers of every other type; he is not less under the authority of Scriptures or less representative of it than the preacher; but his relation to all these authorities is different.

This is most evident in connection with the pastoral director's Scriptural, teaching authority. Community and Scriptures have been brought much more closely together in practice and in theory than was the case in the older view of the minister as preacher. Historical studies have made clear that both under the Old and the New Covenants the people and the book were far more closely associated than was once thought to be the case. Then individual men, personally inspired, were regarded as the original mediators of the Word of God and individual preachers obedient to these writings mediated the Word to men. Now we are aware that frequently the authors and always the editors of the sacred writings were communities which in obedience and by inspiration selected true prophecy from false, genuine gospels from spurious ones, apostolic letters from epistles written by men who had no divine commission. Now it becomes apparent that one cannot know the Scriptures without knowing the community which recorded what it had seen and heard; and that one cannot know the mind of the community without knowing the Scriptures. The result of two centuries of Biblical criticism, as this has affected the thought of the Church, has not been an impairment of the power of the Scriptures but it has been an increase of the sense of the communal character of the book. For this and other reasons the best Biblical preaching going on in the churches today undertakes to interpret the Word of God as a word spoken to Israel and the Church. The minister who is obedient to Scriptures and represents its authority does so as one who is interpreting the mind of the community-before-God. When he undertakes to think with the logic of the community, he does so under the discipline of Scriptures. He must learn to think Biblically if he is to think Christianly. So Scriptural and communal authority begin to fuse but the nature of each changes in the process.

The significance of the communal authority of the minister in our time appears also in his relation to the tradition of the Church. Tradition has assumed a new significance for Protestants in a period dominated by the historical understanding of human life. So long as the Church was understood as primarily institutional, in terms of its parallelism to a state rather than to a cultural society, and so long as tradition meant resistance to reform, conflict between the principles of traditional and Scriptural authority was inevitable. But in our time tradition is conceived otherwise than it was in the sixteenth and eighteenth centuries. It appears in a different form partly because the problem of social continuity has become as great for us as the problem of change and reform, but even more because the historical, cultural character of human existence has come into fuller view. We know tradition now not only in the form of social rigidities resistant to change but as the dynamic structure of modifiable habits without which men do not exist as men. Tradition means a society's language, its conceptual frames of reference, its moral orientation in the world of good and evil, the direction of its science, the selection of the best in its literature and art. We know tradition as a living social process constantly changing, constantly in need of criticism, but constant also as the continuing memory, value system and habit structure of a society. Partly under the influence of comparable movements in a world that has become aware of the significance of tradition in politics and literature, partly under the influence of its own studies and needs, the Church has begun to pay a new attention to its tradition. It sees it not as a dead thing once and for all given for acceptance or rejection, but as living history constantly being renewed, rethought and re-searched for meanings relevant to existing men. The minister of today and tomorrow represents that tradition to a greater or lesser extent. If he knows it and lives in it as the tradition of the great Church he has an authority in the local and the contemporary Christian community which the man who represents only the tradition of a national or denominational or localized community cannot have. If he knows the great tradition he will also know that it is his duty to represent it, interpreting the mind of the Church rather than acting as the representative of a fleeting majority of living and local church members. At worst the effort to exercise this authority becomes a servile representation of old forms, a religious antiquarianism; at its best, however, such communal authority speaks in contemporary language and to contemporary needs out of the long experience and painfully gathered wisdom of the Christian centuries.

It is questionable whether the prominence of communal authority in the new idea of the ministry has special significance for the development of spiritual authority. The latter always remains a highly personal matter; the minister is fitted to exercise this authority by the personal crises through which God leads him. It is conferred upon him only in the inner chamber where ordinary thanksgivings, intercessions, confessions and petitions are daily made and where the extraordinary humblings or clarifications take place. Highly personal, however, as this authority is the experiences out of which it grows can also be affected by the participation of the lonely individual in the life of the whole Church, including its life of prayer.

Whether the minister's institutional authority in Protestantism is being established in our times so that we can speak of the emergence of a clearer idea at this point may remain questionable. American Protestant institutions in general are in flux; the common life of the Protestant church is in part seeking institutional forms through which to express and discipline itself, in part it has developed such forms without officially recognizing their presence, continuing to think in terms of historic structures or polities that do not fit the actual situation and operations of the various agencies. New organizations and activities in the Church are being analyzed with the aid of ancient categories in somewhat the same way that in economic society problems of the distribution of rights to income are discussed with the use of private property concepts applicable to lands and houses but not to stocks, bonds and wages. It seems to be clear that the Church in America in our time like Church in any place at any time is deeply influenced in its institutional forms by the political and economic society with which it lives in conjunction. As the polity of all the churches, whether they are episcopal, presbyterian or congregational by tradition, has been modified in the direction of the political structures of Canada and the United States, so the institutional status and authority of the ministry are being modified in the direction of the democratic type of political, educational and economic executive or managerial authority. In this situation the temptation of ministers to become business managers is balanced by the opposite temptation to maintain the kind of status and authority their predecessors enjoyed in more hierarchically ordered society. The question is not whether the ministry will reflect the institutional forms of leadership in the world but whether it will reflect these with the difference that Christian faith and church life require; whether, in short, the minister will remain "man of God" despite the fact that he is now a director instead of a ruler. Perhaps the kinds of studies that have been made of the art of administration, of the relations of policy and administration, of organization and management in other spheres will be carried forward into the sphere of the Church and may show how much the pastoral director of our time, as pastoral preacher, teacher, counselor and leader of worship has also become the democratic pastoral administrator, that is to say, a man charged with the responsibility and given the authority to hold in balance, to invigorate and to maintain communication among a host of activities and their responsible leaders, all directed toward a common end.

Something has previously been said above about the final point in the emerging new conception of the ministry. The people to whom ministers are sent are first of all the people of the Church but the Church is recognized to be the ministering community whose work is in the world. Hence the minister directs his attention as much toward the "world" as the dean of a medical school has his eye on the potentially and actually sick people of the society outside his closed community of healers, or, to use a wholly different analogy, as much as the mayor of a city keeps in view the nature and the needs of the cultural and economic society of which his city is a center. But the relations of Church and world are as unique as they are constantly changing so that no analogy does justice to the situation. What seems most evident in the case of the modern pastoral director is that he can think of himself neither as parish parson responsible for all the people in a geographic area nor as the abbot of a convent of the saved, but only as the responsible leader of a parish church; it is the Church, not he in the first place, that has a parish and responsibility for it. The minister confronts many of his greatest difficulties at this point, since on the one hand he may lose himself and his ministry among the manifold demands made upon him by the neighborhood, and on the other hand, if he directs his Church as though it had no responsibility for the environing society, he will develop an institution of narrow scope and outlook. Clear understanding of the nature and mission of the Church are prerequisite to any effective solution of the problems that present themselves.

The human needs that the Church exists to meet are much the same at all times. Whether the stars are as near as they seemed to the Psalmist or are removed by the millions and billions of light years to which we must accustom our imagination, still the question is the same: "When I look at thy heavens, the work of thy fingers, the moon and the stars which thou hast established; what is man that thou art mindful of him, and the son of man that thou dost care for him?" (R.S.V.). Whether Israel is exiled by Babylon or a modern people displaced, whether Rachel or a twentieth-century mother mourns for her children they need the same assurance that "your work shall be rewarded. . . . There is hope for your future, . . . and your children shall come back to their own country(R.S.V.)." When the social gospel was at the height its greatest exponent in America, Walter Rauschenbusch, despite his animadversions against traditional religion, saw clearly how much the human problem would remain the same in the best of all possible worlds. He wrote:

In the best social order that is conceivable, men will still smoulder with lust and ambition, and be lashed by hate and jealousy as with the whip of a slave driver. . . . No material comfort and plenty can satisfy the restless soul in us and give us peace with ourselves. . . . The day will come when all life on this planet will be extinct, and what meaning will our social evolution have had if that is all?

We can make far too much of the changing needs of men in changing civilizations. Religion is a highly conservative thing because the fundamental needs of men as finite and delinquent creatures aspiring after infinity and wholeness do not change.

Nevertheless our views of men change somewhat with the

changing forms in which the ultimate dilemmas of existence present themselves. The cry, "What shall I do to be saved?" is made in various ways. At one time it is the cry, "What shall I do to be saved from hell?" At another time, "How can I have a friendly God?" Again men ask, "How can our lives be rescued out of dissipation and dispersion into unity?" It is always the same cry, with the same implications, yet always newly phrased. The form in which it is uttered and heard today is variously interpreted. For T. S. Eliot and the many for whom he speaks it is the cry of salvation from "The Wasteland." For Paul Tillich

[man] experiences his present situation in terms of disruption, conflict, self-destruction, meaninglessness, and despair in all realms of life. This experience is expressed in the arts and in literature, conceptualized in existential philosophy, actualized in political cleavages of all kinds, and analyzed in the psychology of the unconscious. . . . The question arising out of this experience is not, as in the Reformation, the question of a merciful God and the forgiveness of sins; nor is it, as in the early Greek church, the question of infinitude, of death and error; nor is it the question of the personal religious life, or of the Christianization of culture and society. It is the question of a reality in which the self-estrangement of our existence is overcome, a reality of reconciliation and reunion, of creativity, meaning and hope.[6]

The cry for salvation here has become the cry for rebirth. There are others who understand the human situation more in terms akin to those prevailing in certain areas in New Testament days, when it seemed to many men that they were in the control of forces indifferent to their fate and that God, however potentially powerful, was very far off. Not a few men today experience their dilemma as that of creatures who were born to be free

[6] *Systematic Theology*, Vol. I (1951), p. 49.

but are everywhere in chains. Nature for them is a power whose iron laws or chance throws of the dice decide the time and place and race and endowment of the child at birth. History, whether interpreted as the realm of determinism or of chance, moves on its way like a tide carrying individual drops and waves of water to melt into the sands or to disappear on the horizon. Social forces, economic movements, machines and inventions that neither inventors nor statesmen can control, biological movements multiplying populations despite leagues for planned parenthood, psychological powers mysteriously hidden beyond the reach of consciousness—these and many other lesser forces direct the course of life and determine its destiny. And God is a God who hides himself. They are not unbelievers, these men; but for them the dominions, principalities, powers and rulers of the darkness of this world have a reality that makes the difference between ancient and modern mythologies of little importance. The cry for salvation that such men make is the cry for freedom from bondage, or to use a contemporary phrase, from the "other-directedness" and heteronomy of existence, from the life of mass-man.

As it becomes aware of the specific form in which ultimate human problems present themselves in our own time, the ministry, and therewith the schools that prepare men for it, begin to understand more sharply what the pastoral function is, in what language the gospel speaks to this need, and what form the Church must take in serving such men in such a time.

CHAPTER 3

The Idea of a Theological School

I. SEMINARIES IN QUANDARY

The theological schools of the churches in America share all the perplexities of the contemporary Protestant community and its ministry. Though they also participate in the movements toward clarification and reconstruction apparent in the latter the first impression they give is like the one produced by the pluralistic churches and a harried ministry: an impression of uncertainty of purpose. We have, indeed, found in the schools evidence of that pluralism and harassment; for they reflect in the multiplicity of their numbers, the variety of their statements of purpose and the conglomerate character of their courses of study the lack of unity symptomatic of their social context. They are also surely partly responsible for the situation since as educational centers of the Church they are in a better position to modify it than are most other agencies.

Perhaps it is a mistake to say that the first impression given by the theological schools is one of multiplicity and indefiniteness of purpose. The first impression many observers receive is one of inertia and conservatism. Though such successive innovations in theological study as the social gospel, social ethics, religious education, psychological counseling and ecumenical relations may receive much publicity the schools seem to go on their accustomed way, teaching what they have always taught: Biblical and systematic theology, church history and preaching. The adjustments made here and there to meet the demands of changing times and the pressures issuing from alumni and church boards scarcely affect the main tenor of their work. They are like the great majority of ministers in this respect, for the pastors also carry on their traditional functions with only slight modifications despite the stir caused by those who want to change the profession in some revolutionary manner. Yet the apparent conservatism is indicative of perplexity. For in the case of the schools as of the ministers, doing the traditional things does not mean doing them for a traditional reason; nor does it mean that these acts are internally integrated. It is the difference between the repetition of separate, habitual actions and the continuation in novel movements of a historic line of march. So traditionalism in painting repeats the same old themes of portraiture, genre, seascape and landscape in ever sleeker forms; it repeats; it does not move. But in its living tradition that art— moving for instance from Rembrandt through Daumier and Van Gogh to Rouault—brings unitive and fresh perception, contemporaneousness of understanding and inventive technique to the ever-new discovery and revelation of man's and nature's faces and forms. Though it makes its discoveries in the same world in which the conventionalist moves, it is as different from imitative traditionalism as it is from the antitraditionalism that tries to find newness for the sake of novelty itself. Similar distinctions between dead and living tradition may be made in every realm of human workmanship.

So considered the conservatism of the theological schools does betray a certain repetitiveness of individual actions and lack of great unifying conceptions. Usually they teach Bible, theology, church history and preaching as separate subjects. Some few new and again distinct subjects are usually added for the sake of modernization, but the conventional disciplines remain in the ascendant. Each of them is regarded, doubtless rightly, as very important; but why it is important and what its place is in a definable whole eludes the definitions of catalogue writers and apparently of most curriculum committees. Studies in the history, literature and theology of Old and New Testaments occupy a large part of the time of almost all theological students. Why they should do so is rarely clearly understood by them and perhaps only somewhat more frequently by their teachers. That the Bible is very important all Christians understand; but why and in what ways it is important requires explanation. It has always been studied in theological schools and doubtless always will be. The question is not whether it will be studied but with what sense of its unity, in what context and in what relation to other subjects. Neither the medieval nor the sixteenth-century understanding of its significance seems wholly cogent today. Yet no generally accepted new analysis of its meaning has been formulated. If Bible study has become a specialty or series of specialties today the reason is not to be sought simply in the development of specialization among teachers of theology but in the loss of a controlling idea in theological education—an idea able to give unity to many partial inquiries. Similar reflections apply to the other traditional disciplines of the theological schools. What has always been taught is now being taught so far as the elements are concerned;

but one thing previously implicit in all that was taught is not now being transmitted: the unifying idea. Thus the apparent conservatism of the schools is really indicative of uncertainty of aim.

The tendency toward pluralism and the participation of the schools in the confusion of churches and ministers becomes even more apparent in their efforts to add to the traditional core of theological studies new disciplines which are to serve as bridges between the heritage and modern men, or, more immediately, between it and the needs of ministers in modern churches. During the course of the last two or three generations the theological curriculum has been "enriched"—like vitamin-impregnated bread—by the addition of a long series of short courses in sociology and social problems, rural and urban sociology, the theory of religious education, educational psychology, methods of religious education, psychology of religion, psychology of personality, psychology of counseling, methods of pastoral counseling, theory of missions, history of missions, methods of evangelism, theory and practice of worship, public speaking, church administration, et cetera, et cetera. Almost every school catalogue gives evidence of such additions, particularly when it is compared with one of its predecessors from the year 1900. These additions—which have again in part been subtracted—show the great awareness of the schools that they must mediate between the heritage and the contemporary situation. But the way in which such additions have been made also indicates how little guidance schools have received or given in the task of thinking through the whole work of the Church from a unified and unifying point of view, how much they have been caught up in the tendency to respond to varying external pressures and needs without stopping first of all to come to a new self-collectedness. For these courses have been added piecemeal and almost each one of the new specialties has appeared with a new theological rationalization of its existence so that missions, the gospel for society, religious education and pastoral counseling each found itself tempted or compelled to develop its own theology.

The present curriculum of the theological schools in general shows the effects of this development or, rather, lack of development. It may be more unified than most college curricula are but nonetheless it impresses the observer as a collection of studies rather than as a course of study. When he participates in meetings of theological faculties or their curriculum committees his impression is verified by the manner in which requirements for graduation are mathematically calculated and distributed among departments. The lack of unity is also indicated in the efforts that are made to provide for "integration" by adding examinations, theses or interdepartmental courses which will insure that students will combine in their own minds what has been fragmentarily offered them.

Other indications of the lack of a sense of direction in theological education today are to be found in the hidden and open conflicts present in the schools. Such conflicts usually reflect an exaggeration of inevitable tensions that are probably healthful when they are understood, accepted and ordered into a whole life. The tension associated with the nature of the Church as one body with one Head that has many members becomes conflict when the members think themselves self-sufficient and refuse to accept their fellow members as equally related to the Head. In the form of denominationalism that conflict is not as acute today as once it was though there are schools in which the question whether they are to teach church or denominational theology is the unacknowledged background of sharp debates about courses and teachers and there are others that regard themselves and their denominations as the sole guardians of "the truth." Denominationalism, as meaning priority of loyalty to denomination over loyalty to the cause of the Church, appears more frequently in the form of provincialism than of antagonism to others. In its exaggerated form of conflict the tension of members and body seems to appear most often in the antagonisms of liberalism and conservatism or of high and low churchmanship. The sort of liberalism which looks with contempt upon conservative groups and their schools or even on conservative tendencies in theology in general, calling them all "Fundamentalist," and the kind of conservatism that abhors all critical movements alike, cut themselves off from each other in the theological world more effectively than do Baptists from Presbyterians, Methodists from Anglicans.

This antagonism is akin to another, the one between exponents in theology of the self-sufficiency of the Church and exponents of the interdependence of Church and world. Given the polarity of the Church as Church-in-the-world, conflict arises when the polarity is denied either in the refusal of one party to accept itself as part of the Church or the refusal of another to accept the world as the Church's neighbor. Antagonisms of this sort appear in theological education mostly in hidden form, as faculty members debating about the admission of students, about the inclusion or exclusion of courses or about the place of graduate studies in theology, suspect each other of too much worldliness or too much church provincialism. Doubt-less such suspicions may be traced back as far as the college of the apostles and Paul, but our ironic participation in them today still leaves us with the feeling that something else is amiss besides common frailty and sin. What can we assume about one another's ideas of the Church? And if we have no great ideas to which to assent or from which to dissent how can we achieve even compromise?

The constant rivalry between advocates of the "academic," or "content," or "classic" theological courses and promoters of "practical training" presents us with a similar situation. There are few theological schools where these groups do not compete for the students' interest and time, where some members of the former group do not feel that the scholarliness of theolog-ical study is being impaired by the attention claimed for field work and counseling, where teachers of preaching, church ad-ministration and pastoral care and directors of field work do not regard much of the theological work as somewhat beside the point in the education of a minister for the contemporary Church.

Such is the first, superficial impression: our schools, like our churches and our ministers, have no clear conception of what they are doing but are carrying on traditional actions, making separate responses to various pressures exerted by churches and society, contriving uneasy compromises among many values, engaging in little quarrels symptomatic of undefined issues, trying to improve their work by adjusting minor parts of the academic machine or by changing the specifications of the raw material to be treated.

II. SIGNS OF NEW VITALITY

The first, superficial impression is not erased by more thorough acquaintance with theological schools; many instances of self-satisfied provincialism, inert traditionalism and specious modernization tend to confirm it. But more intimate acquaintance also brings into view a second, very different aspect of the scene. Alongside conventionality, which is sometimes downright antiquarian, one encounters vitality, freshness, eagerness and devotedness among these teachers and students, Alongside perplexed preparation for manifold tasks one finds present in many of these men a drive toward knowledge of the essential, a search for central Christian wisdom about the fundamental issues of life. Alongside tepid birthright loyalties to denominations and schools of thought, one encounters in faculty and students the fervent convictions of new converts about the greatness of the common Christian cause. And amidst the confusions and perplexities of many men doing many things only institutionally connected, the sense of the great tradition of the Church emerges in many places as the idea of a line of march to be taken up, of a direction to be followed, a continuing purpose to be served. Though no clear-cut idea of the theological school or of theology as a whole is as yet in prospect, a sense of renewal and promise, a feeling of excitement about the theological task is to be felt in the academic climate and it is accompanied by invigoration of intellectual inquiry and of religious devotion.

Examples of such a spirit—which is always a new spirit however frequently it has manifested itself in the past—may be found in whole schools. It is also represented on almost every faculty, even the most discouraged, by one or two young men or perennially youthful veterans, and in every corps of students, even the most somber assortment of theological-student stereotypes. Our examples, however, may be more wisely chosen from departments of study and types of educational work.

A remarkable thing has happened in recent years to the study of the Old Testament. There was a time, not too remote, when this subject was studied and doubtless sometimes taught with the kind of enthusiasm one associates with high school recitation periods at two o'clock on drowsy days in May. But now the study of the Old Testament has become a fascinating and exciting business in school after school. Students from various institutions speak of the illumination that has come to them from historic yet living participation in Israel's encounters with God, in the sorrows and exaltations, the judgments and deliverances of patriarchs, lawgivers, psalmists and prophets. In explanation of the phenomenon it may be said that an unusually brilliant group of teachers happens to be at work today in this field; yet such reasoning does not carry very far for these teachers had their peers in previous generations. Perhaps the explanation is to be found in the hints some students give of the extent to which the Old Testament has become for them an introduction to the fundamental problems of man's life before God, a revelation of the greatness, freedom and power of the Sovereign Lord, of the meaning of the people of God and of human history. The indications are that many of them came to theological study with a religion so sentimental or so narrowly Christ-centered that it had left them without answers to their deepest questions about the reason for their existence, about the meaning of human tragedy, and the significance of mankind's history. They had accepted what had been told them, but had remained ill at ease. For instance, they had learned that Jesus Christ is the answer to human problems but the Christ to whom they had been introduced was a figure unrelated to the great context in which he appeared and one who left them without answers to many of their personal questions as existing and historical men. In the study of Old Testament they had now been led by their teachers to discover what their human questions were and to what questions Jesus Christ is the answer. If this means that the Old Testament is being taught in such schools today as a part of theology it does not mean that the historical and critical approach to it is ignored or that inspiration and devotion have taken the place of scholarship. It does mean that the books of the Old Covenant are studied in the context of an intellectual love of God and neighbor, of a faith that seeks understanding.

In the case of New Testament studies a similar though less remarkable development is taking place. Partly again because very able theologians are studying and teaching in this field, partly because critical, historical scholarship is being combined with existential awareness of that human dilemma and of that divine grace with which the New Testament writings are concerned, partly for other reasons, vital interest in the meaning of the New Testament is increasing. In this case as in that of the Old Testament there are differences between conservative and liberal seminaries, but in any case it is the New Testament not as literature in general, or as record of the religious experiences of people remotely related to our generation, or as collection of dogmatic statements of right belief, or as an anthology of wise ethical maxims, but as the story of the central event in the divine-human encounter that is being studied.

The concern for theology, not as a particularist discipline but as the search for human wisdom about the wisdom of God in the creation and redemption of man, is manifest in other disciplines besides Biblical studies: in systematic theology frequently, occasionally in Christian ethics, homiletics, religious education and pastoral counseling. This concern is accompanied by great interest in the Church and its relations to culture. Special courses have been introduced in some schools to deal with the nature of the Church, especially in the perspective of the ecumenical movement. New work is also being done in an effort to interpret the religious or Christian meanings found in modern secular literature, philosophy, science and art. But the measure of these interests is not to be taken by counting the number of such special courses. The question is really how courses in Church history, missions and practical theology on the one hand, in systematic theology, Christian ethics and philosophy of religion on the other, are being taught. An impression one gains from many teachers of these subjects as well as from their students, is that often now a robust sense of Church is accompanied by great willingness to enter into conversation with secular society. That conversation is being conducted in no apologetic tone but with the humility and openness of mind possible to those who are not self-defensive and who are neither ashamed of being churchmen nor hostile to the world outside the Church.

Other symptoms of this new spirit are to be found in the increased interest in the common worship of the academic community, though this is by no means universally evident; in the widespread and intensive discussions of faculties about the purpose and organization of the course of study; in the experiments that are being carried on to relate the work of the seminary more intimately to the work of other church agencies, particularly to the local churches.

Yet it remains questionable whether all these movements and interests are leading in one direction, whether such clear principles of unity and of central purpose are being discovered that the schools are now enabled to correlate their particularistic endeavors to prepare men for multiple services in heterogeneous churches. It is clear, of course, that no single pattern will suffice for a church so complex as the Protestant church in America and for schools with so many heritages and responsibilities. Nevertheless, if a common sense of Church is nascent among the many members of one body and if a relatively clear idea is emerging of the one service to be rendered by ministers in their many duties, then some common idea of a theological school ought also to be possible. Such an idea would not be applicable as a blueprint for the reconstruction of the several institutions but only as a kind of general prescription of the elements every blueprint would need to provide for. No single pattern will suffice as a plan for the building of houses adequate to the needs of all American families in our time; their histories and tastes and duties are too various. But any house built today will provide for all the necessary functions of family life with the use of those instruments that modern civilization affords and with consideration of the services that the larger community now makes available to the home. It will also take into account the special form that family life has assumed in modern times while continuing the long tradition of the home. So it is possible to define the idea of a modern dwelling in the abstract while allowing for the infinite variations necessary before that idea can be made specifically useful for a particular family. The question is whether a general idea of a theological school can be formulated which might be comparable to such an abstract modern version of the traditional idea of a dwelling. Any effort to answer that question today in North America cannot undertake to state an apparent and growing consensus. It can only be a somewhat private essay offered for the sake of furthering and drawing together a lively but rather scattered discussion going on among many groups in the one room of the Church.

III. THE CHARACTER AND PURPOSE OF A THEOLOGICAL SCHOOL

We begin that effort by defining the theological school as *intellectual center of the Church's life.* Though anti-intellectualism within the Church and anti-ecclesiasticism among intelligentsia outside it will object to the close correlation of intellect and Church, their ill-founded objections need not detain us. We content ourselves at this stage with the reflections that to love God with the whole understanding has ever been accepted by the great Church, if not by every sect, as part of its duty and privilege; and that there is no exercise of the intellect which is not an expression of love. If love is not directed toward God and neighbor it is directed toward something else, perhaps even toward the intellect itself in the universal tendency toward narcissism.

To speak in Aristotelian language, the efficient, material, formal and final causes of the theological school are identical with those of the Church. Its motivation is that of the Church—

the love of God and neighbor implanted in human nature ₁ₐ₁
creation, redeemed, redirected and invigorated by the acceptance of the good news of God's love for the world. Its membership consists of churchmen: existing and historic individuals,
gathered together in a common life of faith which among other
things seeks understanding of itself, of God and neighbor. Its
form is the form of the Church—the subject before God, the
institution and community, the local and universal, the critical
and constructive companion of the world. Its purpose is the
purpose of the Church—the increase among men of the love
of God and companions.

Of course, the theological school is not Church in its wholeness. It is not even the intellect of the Church; but as an intellectual center it is a member of the body. While intellectual
activity is as widely diffused throughout the whole Church as
are activities of worship and of compassion, there are also centers or occasions of special intellectual activity in it as there are
centers or occasions of special adoration and charity. Wherever
and whenever there has been intense intellectual activity in
the Church a theological school has arisen, while institutions
possessing the external appearance of such schools but devoid
of reflective life have quickly revealed themselves as training
establishments for the habituation of apprentices in the skills
of a clerical trade rather than as theological schools. The intellectual activity of the Church which centers on occasion in a
theological school and for which the theological school bears
responsibility is like all intellectual action yet derives specific
characteristics from the objects toward which it is directed and
from the love that guides it. Like all intellectual activity it compares, abstracts, relates; by these means it seeks coherence in

the manifoldness of human experience, unified understanding of the objects or the Other in that experience. It also undertakes to correct through criticism, false ideas of the Other and inappropriate reactions to it. Like all intellectual activity it is carried on in constant conversation among many subjects, whose ideas of the common object and whose reactions to it are compared, related and criticized. But theology is differentiated from other kinds of intellectual activity by being the reflection that goes on in the Church; it is therefore the kind of thinking that is directed toward God and man-before-God as its objects and which is guided by the love of God and neighbor. Both objectives and motivation are important in distinguishing its special character. Insofar as it is genuine church-thinking it is distinctly different from all intellectual activity guided by love of self or love of neighbor-without-God, or of intellect itself, or of knowledge for its own sake—if there is such a love. Intellectual activity motivated by such interests may indeed make Ultimate Being and man its objects of study and so seem to share in the thought of the Church; but insofar as it is directed by a love that is not love of Being and of man it cannot see or understand what love understands. Theology differs from such modes of thinking about God and man because it is a pure science, disinterested as all pure science is disinterested, seeking to put aside all extraneous, private and personal interests while it concentrates on its objects for their own sake only. On the other hand theology differs from intellectual activities directed toward other objects than God and man-before-God. Such activities may indeed be motivated by the love that animates theology, but they abstract the objects to be understood from the objects of ultimate love, focusing attention on some

part or aspect of creation without making them objects of devotion. Historically theology has not always been aware of the differences between its relations to the former and the latter kinds
of "secular" intellectual activity. Sometimes it has relegated
both sorts to the realm of "worldly" sciences; sometimes it has
presumed to assert its queenship over both though in the course
of that assertion it has itself become worldly, allowing itself to
be guided by self-love or love of the Church, not by the Church's
love. When it follows its own genius it is related to these various
sorts of intellectual activity in the various ways that Church is
related to world.[1] In all relations it is not a queen but a servant,
though its service may at times need to take the form of criticism and polemic.

As center of the Church's intellectual activity, animated by
the Church's motivation and directed by its purpose, the theological school is charged with a double function. On the one
hand it is that place or occasion where the Church exercises its
intellectual love of God and neighbor; on the other hand it is
the community that serves the Church's other activities by
bringing reflection and criticism to bear on worship, preaching,
teaching and the care of souls. Intellectual gifts whether used
in one way or the other are indispensable to the functioning of
the whole community but they are not pre-eminent as intellectu-
alism asserts. There are theological as well as psychological reasons for denying to the idea-forming, abstracting, comparing
and critical work of the mind the kind of superiority to physical
action, imagination, emotion and unconscious operation that
is often claimed for it. All the warnings Paul uttered, and the
Church in principle has accepted, against the tendency of any

[1] See above, p. 33.

function of the body to claim priority over others apply to the relation of intellectual to other activities. But granted that "heart and soul and strength," or feeling and intuition and will, or sentiment, the unconscious depths and physical vitality, are all to be employed in exercising love to God and man, yet the "mind"—intelligence and understanding—also has its rightful, indispensable place in the economy of human and of Church life. Though intellectual love of God and neighbor is not the supreme exercise of love, yet it is required and possible since man is also mind and does not wholly love his loves if his mind does not move toward them. He cannot truly love with heart, soul and strength unless mind accompanies and penetrates these other activities as they in turn accompany and penetrate it. The coldness of an intellectual approach unaccompanied by affection is matched by the febrile extravagance of unreasoning sentiment; the aloofness of uncommitted understanding has its counterpart in the possessiveness of unintelligent loyalty. When the whole man is active the mind is also active; when the whole Church is at work it thinks and considers no less than it worships, proclaims, suffers, rejoices and fights.

The theological school is the center where both types of intellectual activity are carried on: the kind that, supported by other actions, moves directly toward the objects of the Church's love and the kind that supports the other movements toward those objects. The theological school in this way is like any other intellectual center where both "pure" and "applied science" are pursued, with the proviso that these phrases are misnomers for the intricate interaction of the science that confines its interest to its object only and the science whose disinterestedness in personal and private concerns is disciplined by interest in humanity. As pure science theology is that response of man's nascent love toward God and neighbor which seeks to know the beloved, not with the question whether it is worthy of love, but with wonder; not for the sake of power over the beloved but as overpowered. Or, speaking by reference to the end rather than the beginning, it is the movement of the mind toward the hoped-for God and the hoped-for neighbor. This is not to say, as some philosophers do, that thinking itself is worship of God; an element of worship is present, to be sure, in all objective thinking but the worship may be that of an idol or the sort of self-worship which desecrates the object of thought by making it a means to the end of self-glorification. It is to say, however, that thinking may be truly worshipful, and that theology is not only ancillary to other actions of the Church but is itself a primary action. Such a movement of the mind toward God and the neighbor-before-God is characteristic of the Church in all its parts but it is the first duty and a central purpose of the theological school.

From everything that has been said it should be clear that theology so considered as a pure science does not have as its object God in isolation. The word "theology" in its literal sense as the science of God is as applicable and inapplicable to the intellectual activity of the Church as the word "medicine" is to the studies of the healing community. The God who makes himself known and whom the Church seeks to know is no isolated God. If the attribute of *aseity*, i.e., being by and for itself, is applicable to him at all it is not applicable to him as known by the Church. What is known and knowable in theology is God in relation to self and to neighbor, and self and neighbor in relation to God. This complex of related beings is the object of theology. In the great, nearly central figure of Christianity, the God-man, this complex appears at least symbolically, though theology is distorted if it is converted into Christology. The nature of theology is most pertinently expressed by the Thomist and Calvinist insistence: "True and substantial wisdom principally consists of two parts, the knowledge of God and the knowledge of ourselves. But while these two branches of knowledge are so intimately connected, which of them precedes and produces the other, is not easy to discover." To the present writer it seems better to say that true and substantial wisdom consists of three parts: the knowledge of God, of companions, and of the self; and that these three are so intimately related that they cannot be separated. For self-knowledge and knowledge of the other, even though the other be the human neighbor, remain two different things. This point, however, is not necessary in our argument which is simply that theology has as its complex object God in his relations to the self with its companions, and the self with its companions in their relations to God. With this object the reflections and experiences of the Bible deal, with it the great theologians were concerned. It is only broken into parts for convenience as when Christian ethics as study of man is separated from systematic theology as reflection about God. What this definition of the object of theology means for the organization of theological studies cannot here be developed. What is at issue is the reflection that theology as a "pure science," motivated by love of its object, is directed always toward both God and man, or that as intellectual activity it is subject to the double commandment of love of God and neighbor. The proper study of mankind is God and man-before-God in their interrelation.

The second function of theology as the intellectual activity of the Church and so of the theological school as a center of this activity, is the service of other activities of the Church through the exercise of theoretical understanding. Worship unreflected upon, not understood in its relations to God and to other service of God, or in its relations to works of discipline and mercy, or in its context in the whole life and history of the community, uncriticized in its perversions, tends to become habitual repetition of rites; it becomes magical or theurgistic, or is impoverished by sectarian or temporal rejection of the heritage of the whole community. The worshiper and especially the leader of worship needs not only to worship but to know what this action means in the complex of all his doings, of all the deeds of the Church and of the deeds of God. The worshiping Church needs a theology of worship not as preliminary or as addition to, but as accompaniment of, its action. So also in the case of preaching and teaching. The proclamation of the good news of divine love, of the forgiveness of sin and the deliverance from evil; exhortation to lead the Christian life; instruction of young and old in the Christian faith—these evidently require not only that the minister have heard and apprehended the gospel, comprehended the law and learned the creed, but that he have gained insight into the ways of God and men and that he grow continually in his understanding of them; that further he have grasped the meaning of preaching and teaching in relation to all the other activities he and the Church carry on. The care and cure of souls requires theological comprehension in the broad sense of the word "theology." Psychological understanding of self and other men, sociological perception of the communal setting in which individuals suffer, sin, grow guilty, anxious and despairing, the human empathy and sympathy needed by the men of the Church as they seek to help the needful—these must all be united, informed and transformed by theological understanding of man-before-God and God-with-man if the work of the counselor is to be the work of the Church. The building of the Church as a community with complex organizational structure, with manifold functions and leaders, with various responsibilities to the society around it, can easily degenerate into the building of religious clubs, of sororities and fraternities and of national associations for the promotion of good causes, if the understanding of the Church's purpose, of its responsibility to God, of the nature and action of God, of man and his history, of the meaning of the Church's work in all the complex of human activity and of the interrelation of the various aspects of its work are lost to view.

The need for theological understanding and criticism on the part of the preacher and teacher has always been understood, perhaps especially by the churches of the Reformation though it is probably no accident that theological studies in the Roman Church have been especially developed in times past by the preaching orders. The need for theological preparation and continuous study on the part of the priest or leader of worship and the pastoral counselor has not always been as clearly recognized and these functions of the Church have suffered in consequence. Today, if it is true as has been previously suggested, that the work of the minister centers in his activity as pastoral director of a church, the necessity for profound understanding of the meaning of the Church but particularly of that reality to which it points in all its action seems to be very evident. As a general physician needs a knowledge of the structure, functioning and pathology of a whole psychosomatic person in his physical, so-cial environment; as a statesman needs to understand the con-stitution, the dynamics, the history, the value system, the social evils, and the international relations of the society he governs, so the pastoral director of a church needs to know the nature, the purpose, the relations, the structure, the history, the defor-mations, and the responsibilities of the Church. And no such understanding is possible apart from knowledge of God before whom and for whom the Church exists, and apart from knowl-edge of man in his responsibility to God.

A theological school, then, is that center of the Church's intellectual activity where such insight into the meaning and relations of all the Church's activities is sought and communi-cated. It is sought there first of all by those who are preparing to assume responsibility for the Church's work. The theological school is a place where young men are taught to understand the world of God in which the Church operates and the operations of the Church in that world, but it is clear that they cannot be taught unless those who teach them as well as they themselves are constantly in quest of such understanding. It is also, how-ever, the place whither maturer leaders of the Church resort for longer and shorter periods of intensive intellectual work in a community of intellectual workers.

How a theological school so defined as intellectual center of the Church's life differs from a trade school, from a bookish center where not understanding of God and man but of books is sought, from a school of philosophy, a Bible school, a school for preachers, a monastery, et cetera, does not need to be de-scribed in detail. We shall need, however, to inquire into the chief methods by which theological understanding is gained.

IV. THE THEOLOGICAL COMMUNITY

An intellectual center of the Church's life which serves the purposes of theological activity necessarily has the form of a college, that is of a *collegium* or colleagueship. It is a community of students in communication with one another, with the common subjects or objects studied, and with companions of the past and present in like communication with the objects. Every genuine school is such a society in which the movement of communication runs back and forth among the three—the teacher, the student and the common object. When communication is a one-way process, proceeding from an authoritative person to an immature learner who is not in direct relation to the object of the study, intellectual activity is at a minimum in both parties; such a school is not a community of students but a propaganda or indoctrination institution. The study of nature is unreal when textbooks and purely verbal communication take the place of laboratories so that natural entities or activities are not the instructors of both tutors and pupils. In view of the nature of the common object of theology—God and man in their interrelations—it is particularly evident that the intellectual community cannot be bi-polar, consisting only of teachers and students. It is even more dependent than the scientific community on the direct relation of the knowers to theological reality—the God of faith and believing men, the subjects and objects of ultimate love, the commander and the commanded, the forgiver and sinner. Indeed the infinitely active and inexhaustible nature of the subjects of theology reduces to relatively small significance the distance between the more and less mature members of the community of inquiry. Teachers and students form one group before their common objects, which are, indeed, subjects, actively making their presence felt in the community.

The presence in the theological community of the ultimate objects or subjects of study, like its engagement in serving the ultimate purpose of the Church, means that theological students are personally involved in their work to an unusual degree. The study of the determination of personal and human destiny by the mystery of being beyond being, of the tragedy and victory of the son of man, of the life-giving, healing power immanent in personal and social existence, of the parasitic forces of destruction that infest the spiritual as well as the biological organism, of the means of grace and the hope of glory—this cannot be carried on without a personal involvement greater than seems to be demanded by the study of history, nature or literature. If students are not personally involved in the study of theology they are not yet studying theology at all but some auxiliary science such as the history of ideas or ancient documents. Hence theological study is hazardous; the involvement may become so personal and emotional that intellectual activity ceases and the work of abstraction, comparison and criticism stops. Other hazards appear because intellectual activity requires that the objects of ultimate concern in the study be often set at the fringe of awareness while ideas and patterns, forms and relations are put in the center. The avoidance of temptations that arise in this situation will need to concern us later. The point to be insisted on here is that the theological community is constituted not by teachers and learners but by these and the subjects of their common inquiry.

In other respects also it is necessary to think of the theological enterprise in terms of community and as an affair of genuine back-and-forth communication. The course of study is a course of constant conversation with members of a wide circle of men who live in community with God and with neighbors-before-God. The necessary introduction to Christian theology is through Biblical studies and these need to occupy the theologian throughout his work, whatever be his specialty. But Biblical studies are in essence participation in the life of the Biblical communities that found their source and their focus in God. To study the Bible is not to study impersonal writings, Utopian ideas, heavenly patterns. It is to participate in the life of Israel and the early Church, in their hearing and interpretation of the Word spoken through all the sounds that assailed their ears, in their obedience and disobedience to the Will beyond all wills, in their mindfulness and understanding of the mighty acts of ultimate judgment and deliverance in all the arbitraments and liberations of history. It is to share in their appeals for mercy, in their questionings and reasonings with God, in their disputes, disagreements and reconciliations among themselves. There is no other way to learn, organize and apprehend experience, think and speak Christianly, than by long and continuous participation in the life of the Biblical communities. In this conversation with those who being dead yet speak we learn the logic as well as the language of the community that centers in God. Whatever the discontinuities between Israel and the early Church on the one hand, the modern Church on the other so far as their participation in natural, cultural and political events go, fundamental continuity prevails so far as divine-human and interhuman relations before God are concerned. For, as was pointed out previously, the knowledge of

God and man with which we are concerned in the Church is precisely the knowledge available to those who stand in this historic community and apprehend reality from its point of view. In this communication between the Biblical and the modern communities the movement is not all one way; it is not simply the Bible that speaks to the theological student; he also speaks to the men of the Bible. Nothing is more evident from the history of Biblical interpretation in the Church and from the self-critical conversations of modern Biblical scholars than that the movement is reciprocal. New light does break forth from Scriptures as inquirers learn from their social and personal experience to ask new questions of the old communities and to read apparently familiar communications in a new setting. Every classical literature possesses such power of continuing its life and of developing new meanings in the minds of those who study not only it but the realities with which it deals. So Plato and Aristotle, Aeschylus and Virgil, Dante and Shakespeare continue to play active roles in Western cultural society. Far more than they, Moses and Isaiah, the Psalmists, Paul and John, Matthew, Mark and Luke participate in the life of the modern Christian community.

The theological community includes also the men and societies of Christian history. The Reformers, to be sure, revolted against the dominance of tradition at the expense of the Bible. The Reformation both established the priority of Biblical studies and tended to exclude from the theological community the theologians, prophets and churchmen of the post-New Testament period. It seemed sufficient that theology should combine with the present questionings of men in encounter with God and neighbors intense participation in the life of the men of Scriptures. In fact, however, tradition became established again as soon as it was banished. The second generation of Protestant theological students attended at least to Luther's and Calvin's words about attending to the Word of God. There is no Bible school or Biblical seminary that does not also study the mind of some founder of its method of interpreting Scripture, or of some other groups of Bible students besides itself. The question is not really whether the theological community should include only immediately present human beings and the men of Scriptures; other, historic men and groups will always be included. The question is how representative of the whole Church these men and societies will be, whether the Augustines and Thomases, not to speak of the Senecas and Ciceros, who belonged to the Reformers' community of discourse are to be heard directly; whether the response of Christians to the fall of the Roman Empire is to be understood or only their response to the decay of medieval civilization; whether the thirteenth-century revival of the Church or only its eighteenth-century awakening is to be regarded; whether only the fathers of a denomination or also the Church fathers on whom they relied are to be included in the community of discourse.

The study of historical theology and of the historical Church, whatever the limits within which it is undertaken, is as necessary as it is an inevitable part of theological inquiry. Under the influence of theories of progress or decline or development in history such study has frequently been carried on for the purpose of explaining the differences between Biblical and modern life before God. But, in effect, historical study is always far more important than these patterns of interpretation indicate. What happens in it is that men and communities of the past, confronting strange situations, making new responses and mistakes, yet always concerned with the one God and the same Christ, are included in the conversation of the present theological society. In this conversation chronological priority and posteriority are often unimportant. Augustine's reflections may be more illuminative of the common subject than the later ideas of Thomas Aquinas; Luther may answer more questions of the modern student about his puzzling situation in guilt and anxiety before God than Schleiermacher; Bernard of Clairvaux may clarify the meaning of the love of God and neighbor more than a twentieth-century theologian. Historical study in theology, when theology is directed toward its chief objects, is always more like a conversation with a large company of similarly concerned and experienced men than like the tracing of a life history, whatever values there are in the latter procedure. But a theological inquiry that narrows the historical community, that excludes from the conversation such men as the early Fathers of the Church, or the medieval theologians, or the Reformers, or the sectarians of the sixteenth and seventeenth centuries, or the Puritans, Pietists and social gospelers, or such movements as monasticism, scholasticism, Biblicism, et cetera impoverishes itself from the beginning. The study of history is never only the effort to understand the past, or even to understand the human present that has grown out of the past; it is an extension of the effort to understand objects and situations common to the past and the present. It always involves a kind of resurrection of the minds of predecessors in the community of inquiry, and an entering into conversation with them about the common concern.

The principle of communication applies also to the relations of the theological school to other groups and activities in the contemporary Church. The isolated school, out of touch with other intellectual centers of the Church, out of touch also with the worshiping, serving, educating Church, uncognizant of and uninfluenced by the work of the preachers, priests, pastoral counselors and pastoral directors, uncritical and uncriticized, is not an intellectual center of the Church but only of some academic or religious sect. In such a school only fragments of theology can be studied; its partial views are never corrected or illuminated from other perspectives than its own.

Finally, the theological community as a Church center is always in companionship with the "world" and in communication with secular learning. In its participation in the life of the Biblical communities it participates with them in their conversation and conflict with ancient cultures; in its re-enactment of the life of the Church in history it also re-enacts the conversations of theologians with Platonists and Neo-Platonists, with Aristotelians and Averroists, with idealists and realists; it recapitulates the encounters of the institutional Church with Church-reforming and Church-deforming states, of the Christian community with rising and declining cultures. In its dialogue with contemporary churchmen it is involved in their engagements with the metropolitan, industrial society of our time. As center of the contemporary Church's intellectual activity it is also directly responsible for continuous conversation with the intellectual centers of secular society. Its relations to the philosophies, sciences and humanities studied in the latter will be as various as are the relations of the Church to its companion, the world. At times the conversation will be debate and polemic, but even conflict is creative for a theology that has been cured of defensiveness by the faith that infuses it. Frequently the relations will be co-operative, as when views of human nature developed in secular centers illuminate areas inaccessible, though highly germane, to theological understanding, or when the latter supplies insights otherwise unattainable.

This responsibility of the theological school for intercommunication with the world is not discharged by its requirement that those who wish to participate in its work must have previously received a liberal education. Theological inquiry is not something that can be added to humanistic and naturalistic studies. It needs to be constantly informed by them and to inform them. Hence also this responsibility is not met merely by the addition to theological studies of courses in the old or the new humanities—the study of literature, history and philosophy on the one hand, of culture, psychology and sociology on the other. The question is never one of adding bodies of knowledge to each other but always one of interpenetration and conversation. A theological school that is closely related to a university may be in a more favorable situation to maintain connection with humanistic and scientific studies than is the isolated school. It can also more readily make to the body of human learning the contributions that are required of theology. But proximity to a university, even organizational connection with one, does not guarantee that this interchange will take place, nor does distance from such an institution prevent the lively conversation of theology with other disciplines of thought.

This outline of the aspects of theological community activity offers no prescription for the manner in which duties are to be distributed among the members of a school. The division of labor in any society, including the theological school, will always doubtless be somewhat arbitrary. But whatever convenience and expediency require about the way in which the unity of theological study be broken up into manageable parts, the first requirements laid on all the specialists in the community seem to be: that their intellectual participation in the life of the Biblical, the historic and the contemporary Church always have in view the common theological object—God and man in their interrelations; and that it always be carried on in acute awareness of the "world" in which the Church has been assigned its task. One may say that the complex object of theological study always has the three aspects of God in relation to man, of men in relation to God, and of men-before-God in relation to each other, while the method of such study consists of intensive participation in the life of the Biblical, historical and contemporary churches in their encounters with God and interactions with the "world."

V. THEORY AND PRACTICE

Our reflections on the nature of a theological school and on its methods of study have emphasized the theoretical character of its work. Whether its function as the exercise of the intellectual love of God and man or as the illumination of other church activities is stressed, in either case the work of the school is theoretical. As intellectual center of the Church's life it is the place where in specific manner faith seeks understanding. As guide of the immature it seeks to lead them to a knowledge of the whole complex of action in which they are to act; as illuminator and critic the school endeavors to aid the Church to understand what it is doing and by understanding to modify or redirect these actions. Hence it deals with the theory of preaching, of Christian education, of social action and of worship as well as with the theory of divine and human nature, of God's activity and man's behavior. So its work is theoretical through and through.

Objections to this emphasis will arise in various quarters. It will be pointed out that in the past great cleavages between theology and the Church have resulted from a one-sided interest in theory; that the development of the schools, particularly in America during the past hundred years, has been in reaction to the dominance of theory; that the Church needs men who have been practically trained in its work. These objections have some cogency, yet it may be questioned whether they are not directed against a kind of theorizing very different from the sort that has been described and whether they in turn have not led to practices that now stand in need of criticism. This problem of theory and practice which arises in many other contexts in theological schools itself needs theoretical illumination. Though our difficulties in the development of the schools have arisen in part from failure to achieve adequate understanding of our ultimate purposes and our total activity, they seem also to be partly due to inadequate theories of the relations of action and reflection.

Two views of this relation seem to guide and by their antagonism to perplex us. According to the intellectualist theory all human action begins with theory, with an understanding of ideas presented to the mind; the movement is from idea to action, from thought to voluntary deeds. First, it is supposed, we conceive the idea of God, then move toward love and obedience and faith; first we conceive the idea of salvation, then accept this healing work; first we understand the nature of the

Church, then proceed to increase and edify it. Directly opposed to this view is the pragmatic theory which regards theoretical activity as an affair of rationalizations, essentially irrelevant to practice; practice is valued both for its own sake and as more directly contributory than thought can be to the welfare of men and the glory of God. The contention between advocates of these two theories of the relations of theory and practice becomes, in theological schools as well as elsewhere, a debate between two kinds of practitioners—the practitioners of theoretical activity on the one hand, of nontheoretical on the other. But in the course of the debate it becomes apparent that a host of issues is involved, not a simple and definable single issue. In consequence members of what seemed to be two parties are forever changing sides and confusion is increased rather than diminished.

Neither an intellectualist nor a pragmatic understanding of the relations of theory and practice has been presupposed in our definition of the theological school as the center of the Church's intellectual activity and as the college in which the Biblical, the historical and the contemporary Church are included in one community of discourse. What has been implied is the conviction that reflection and criticism form an indispensable element in all human activity, not least in the activities of the Church, but that such reflection cannot be independent of other activities, such as worship, proclamation, healing, et cetera. Reflection is never the first action, though in personal and communal life we can never go back to a moment in which action has been unmodified by reflection. Even when we prevision an act, such as worship, and reflect on what we have not yet done, the act contemplated does not grow out of the contemplation; its sources in the complex human soul are more various. Reflection precedes, accompanies and follows action but this does not make it the source or end of action. Reflection as a necessary ingredient in all activity is neither prior nor subservient to other motions of the soul. Serving these it is served by them in the service of God and neighbor or of the self. It serves them in its own way, by abstracting and relating, by discerning pattern and idea, by criticism and comparison. It is served by a will that disciplines, a love that guides, by the perception of incarnate being, by hope of fulfillment.

The work of a theological school is necessarily reflective but if it is carried on in complete abstraction from other action, or if it is reflection on the actions of other men only, it soon becomes theory in the bad sense of the term—a vision of reflections of reflections. The theoretical work of the intellect needs to be carried on in the context of the Church's whole life; hence those whose special duty it is to do this work must participate in that life if they are to discharge their peculiar duty. One cannot understand the meaning of preaching in the total work of the Church apart from direct personal hearing and proclamation of the gospel, nor know the character of worship, its direction, the requirements it makes on the self and its relations to proclamation and service unless one is a worshiper. How shall one understand Christian education in theory without engaging in it as teacher and student, or church administration without participation in the organized common life of a Christian community? The point is not that we learn by doing. Sometimes we learn nothing by doing except the bare deed, as when children are taught to read by being required simply to read but never learn that written words refer to a whole world beyond them or when theological students are taught to "preach" by being required to make public addresses but never discover the difference between a sermon and an oration. The point is rather that we do not learn the meaning of deeds *without* doing. If action unexamined, unreflected upon and uncriticized is not worth doing, examination, reflection and criticism which are not the self-examination, the self-reflection and self-criticism of a living agent also are scarcely worth carrying on.

A second equally or more important reason why theological study must be set in the context of the Church's whole activity if it is to be genuine theology, lies in the nature of theoretical activity. The intellect abstracts, compares, conceptualizes; it notes relations and forms ideas of them. In theology it turns to ideas of being, of God, of fatherhood and sonship, of sovereignty and mercy, of judgment and salvation. It turns from selves in their concrete personal and communal existence to ideas of the image of God in man, of the soul, of mankind, the people of God, of sin and blessedness. Endeavoring to understand the Church it tries to discern its pattern and to see analogies between churchly and other realities. Now the proper work of the intellect lies in the accurate, critical discovery, definition and testing of such ideas. But this work of theory cannot stand alone because it is a work of abstraction that proceeds from, and must return to, the concrete reality of life. Moreover, engagement in theological inquiry involves the student in personal hazards because he is tempted to regard the abstract as the real and even to make it the object of his love. This danger can be avoided only if theology is set within the larger personal and social context of a life of love of God and neighbor.

While it is true, as has been said before, that theology requires personal involvement on the part of its students, the fact cannot be ignored that in the activity of the intellect the ultimate objects and subjects of love, faith and hope must be set somewhat at the fringe of awareness. In the moment of his study God and neighbor are not present to the theologian as *Thous* addressing or being addressed by this *I*. What is immediately present are forms, patterns, ideas ingredient in the *Thous*. Furthermore, the mind that contemplates ideas is not the self in its whole concrete character with its anxieties and hopes, its highly personal guilt and need of deliverance from evil but rather a kind of common mind, an abstracted self. In the terms Martin Buber has made familiar, theology is an affair of *I-It* rather than of *I-Thou* relations, and the *I* in this *I-It* relation differs from the *I* in the *I-Thou* relation. To be sure, theology does not think of God as an *It* nor does it make a thing out of the neighbor, but the abstractions it attends to are *its*, *things*, rather than selves in their living power. Sin and salvation do not become ideas; but ideas of sin and salvation do occupy the foreground of attention. Neither is the self reduced to the studious, mental self; yet the vocation of the student takes a certain precedence for the time being over the man who among many other things also studies. Because intellectual work requires such attention to the impersonal therefore it is necessary that it be constantly corrected and made serviceable by activities of another sort, especially by the worship of God, the hearing of his Word, and direct service of the neighbor. In worship and in the hearing of the proclamation the eternal *Thou* and the concrete selfhood of worshiper or hearer of the Word are in a confrontation never actualized in study. In the service of the neighbor not only he as a real person but the self also, in all its weakness and need, with all its concrete obligations, are brought into awareness in a manner never achievable by a student of theology so far as he remains a student. Hence while a community which centers in worship is not a theological school, a theological school in which worship is not a part of the daily and weekly rhythm of activity cannot remain a center of intellectual activity directed toward God. Preaching and hearing the proclamation is not theological study; but if students of theology, in all their degrees of immaturity and maturity, do not attend to the Word addressed to them as selves their study represents flight from God and self. A community of service to men is not as such a theological center; but a school that only studies man-before-God and man in relation to neighbor without the accompaniment of frequent, direct encounter with human *Thous*, serving and being served, has become too irresponsible to neighbors to be called a divinity school.

Consideration of the relations of study to worship, to the preaching and hearing of the Word, and to the service of men calls our attention to the significance of these activities as they need to be carried on by the theological community itself. But it also puts into a frequently neglected perspective the meaning of participation by students and faculty in the Church's work outside the confines of the school. All too often "field work" (why not call it "church work?") is regarded and directed as though its purpose were the acquisition of skills for future use. Students, it seems, should teach Sunday School classes because sometime in the future they will need to organize Sunday Schools; to do "clinical work" in hospitals because they will learn something beneficial for their later practice as counselors;

to practice preaching so that in other times and other places they may proclaim divine righteousness and mercy. When such considerations are urged upon them an inner contradiction comes to appearance; a kind of professionalized self-love has been substituted for love of God and neighbor. The children in the Sunday School class, the patients in the hospital, the hearers of the "practice sermon" have been put into a secondary place; they have become means to a personal end. Fortunately, the situations in which students so sent into "field work" find themselves, their own sensitiveness and the grace of God active in many secondary agencies counteract the influence of the theory that such participation in the Church's work is self-loving preparation for the exercise of future other-loving action. It demands immediate self-forgetful service of others; it puts into the center of attention God on whom the servant is dependent and the neighbor who is in need of service. It requires the young man or woman engaging in it to be a minister now, rather than to look forward merely to future ministry. It puts the intellectual love of God and neighbor into the rich context of the present moment. Doubtless participation in church work by students of theology has educational value, since devoted and intelligent men are bound to learn from experience, especially if they can compare it with that of others. But neither self-education nor the undergirding of intellectual activity constitutes the purpose of work that can have only the glory of God and the welfare of companions as its ends. These and other considerations underscore the significance of participation in church work by those who are engaged in theological study. It is important that their studies be set in the context of the Church's work not simply because theology is thereby enriched, but also because it is not a way of life and because a person is not definable in terms of his vocation even though it be the vocation of theological student. Theology is only the intellectual part of a way of life and the young person's problem is not simply one of attaining intellectual comprehension but of growing up into the measure of the stature of the fullness of Christ.

Yet all this does not mean that the theological school should turn away from its own proper work of intellectual activity. It means that theoretical activity can be only provisionally and partly separated from the Church's total action, or that as the theological community is necessary to the functioning of the Church so also the Church's other agencies are necessary to that community. Once more the old parable of the body and its members finds its application.

These adumbrations of the idea of a theological school will seem to some who have followed the course of our argument to be so general or so Utopian as to be irrelevant to the existing seminaries in the United States and Canada. How shall administrators and teachers gain help from such generalities as they struggle to find answers to pressing questions about the extension of the curriculum to four years, about the place in it of Greek and Hebrew, about making better provisions for the theological education and employment of young women? Such questions cannot be answered on the basis of a general idea of theological study without further theoretic inquiry into the specific situations in which they arise.[2] But the problem of

[2] A further volume on theological education in the United States and Canada, now in preparation by the staff of the study project, will come to closer grip with some specific problems.

theological education, as it presents itself to administrators, boards and faculties, does not consist simply of a series of detailed questions. It is also a problem of the over-all goal and context of the seminaries' work. The reflections here offered on that subject have not been developed in abstraction from the practice of theological education but only in some abstraction from the confusion of many details. The idea has been worked out in the midst of practice and in consultation with hundreds of fellow practitioners.

Like every such theory, like theology itself, it remains incomplete and open. It is an effort to understand in the moment, while the conversation in the Church continues, what are the intelligible outlines of the structure of theological study in the Protestant schools. A theological education which does not lead young men and women to embark on a continuous, ever-incomplete but ever-sustained effort to study and to understand the meanings of their work and of the situations in which they labor is neither theological nor education. Similarly, a theory of theological study which does not lead toward new endeavors toward better, more precise and more inclusive understanding of the nature of theological endeavor under the government of God is not a theory of theology but a dogmatic statement backed by no more than individual authority, that is, by no authority at all.

UNIVERSITY OF MINNESOTA

⤥ *Reinhold Niebuhr*

BY NATHAN A. SCOTT, JR.

UNIVERSITY OF MINNESOTA PRESS • MINNEAPOLIS

NATHAN A. SCOTT, JR., is associate professor of theology and literature at the University of Chicago. Among his books are *Modern Literature and the Religious Frontier* and *Albert Camus*.

↗ Reinhold Niebuhr

Man has always been his most vexing problem. How shall he think of himself?" These are the opening lines of the Gifford Lectures which Reinhold Niebuhr delivered at the University of Edinburgh in the spring and autumn of 1939, and they announce the unifying theme of all his thought and writing since the early 1920's, when he first appeared on the national scene as the young pastor of a Detroit congregation of the Evangelical Synod who was projecting a critique of both religion and modern culture more radical than anything that had yet emerged from liberal Protestantism. What is the proper estimate of man? This has been Niebuhr's fundamental question. As he said in his Gifford Lectures, "The obvious fact is that man is a child of nature, subject to its vicissitudes, compelled by its necessities, driven by its impulses, and confined within the brevity of the years which nature permits its varied organic form, allowing them some, but not too much, latitude. The other less obvious fact is that man is a spirit who stands outside of nature, life, himself, his reason and the world." He stands, in other words, at a point of juncture between nature and spirit: he is subject to all the brutal contingencies of nature and history; and yet, in the incalculable reaches of his freedom, he has the capacity to stand outside the forces of nature and to subdue them to his purposes. And not only does man's radical freedom permit him to transcend the necessities of nature and every concretion of historical circumstance: he can also transcend himself, making himself the object of his own knowledge, of his own judgment and forgiveness — and deception. When the full human truth

5

is collapsed into some simplistic formula that overstresses either man's uniqueness and dignity or his affinity with the world of nature and his misery, then the consequence, inevitably, is a fatuous irrelevance to the real complexity of things. This is the fundamental insight that is at the core of Reinhold Niebuhr's entire thought, and it has provided the controlling principle of the theological work and the brilliant forays into social and political criticism that have made him a figure of commanding importance in American intellectual life for the past thirty years.

In an autobiographical essay published in 1956, Niebuhr speaks of the central interest of his life as having been "the defense and justification of the Christian faith in a secular age, particularly among what Schleiermacher called Christianity's 'intellectual despisers.'" And this has indeed been the principal focus of his career. But, unlike Schleiermacher at the beginning of the nineteenth century, Niebuhr has not approached the characteristic intellectual expressions of his age from the premise that *anima humana naturaliter Christiana*; and thus he has not understood his task to be one of identifying what is already proximately Christian in the major secular philosophies of the modern period with which the Christian faith finds itself in contention: the field of "apologetics" has not, in other words, in its traditional form, provided the basic emphasis of his thought and writing. Like his distinguished European colleagues in theology, Emil Brunner and Karl Barth, his deepest conviction has been that the Christian estimate of man is truer and profounder than any secular alternatives, whether classical or modern; and his chief concern has therefore been to accomplish such a transvaluation of modern secularity as might disarm his contemporaries into a fresh apprehension of the cogency and relevance to their condition of the analysis of the human quandary that is implicit in Biblical faith. Thus the proponent of the Christian faith, in proving alternative faiths to be inadequate, seeks to induce the confession: "Lord, to whom shall we go? Thou hast the words of eternal life."

But Niebuhr has also wanted to keep a lively awareness of "the falsehoods and corruptions which may use a final truth as their instrument in actual history." The genuinely prophetic cast of his mind has always kept him alert to the necessity of bringing "the judgment of Christ to bear as rigorously on the household of faith as upon the secular and the pagan world, even as the prophets of Israel were as severe in mediating the divine judgment upon Israel as upon Babylon." In this connection, he has been particularly critical of two recurrent temptations in the history of the Church — the one to establish as an absolute some special *status quo* in the social or economic order in the name of the eternal verities of faith; and the other to take up an obscurantist attitude toward the intellectual disciplines of culture.

Indeed, it is his stringently iconoclastic stance — vis-à-vis at once Schleiermacher's "cultured despisers of religion" and his "religious despisers of culture" — that has conditioned Niebuhr toward a way of doing theology that is essentially polemical. And it is this penchant for polemic that has kept him from producing the kind of serenely architectonic system of theology that has been possible for a Protestant thinker like Paul Tillich or such a Catholic theologian as Lionel Thornton. The whole texture and drive of his thought are "dialogical"; for him, Christianity wins the deepest kind of self-knowledge only as it risks the rough-and-tumble of radical encounter with its chief competitors. In his own work, he has never had any great predilection for the stricter forms of systematic theology.

It is also Niebuhr's tendency to conceive the work of Christian theology in polemical terms that makes it exceedingly difficult for his interpreters to specify the genre that most accurately describes the rich and enormous body of his published work. Is he primarily a specialist in the application of theological perspectives to the issues of social ethics? Is he properly viewed in the terms in which he is regarded by men like Walter Lippmann and Hans Morgenthau and George Kennan and by many secular intellectuals, as one whose principal role has been that of practical strategist and theoretical interpreter of politics? Or do others, such as Arthur Schlesinger, Jr., and Charles Frankel and Will Herberg, reach a better vantage point in more spaciously conceiving his role as that of philosopher of history? These are undoubtedly all views that are arguable and that are indeed partially validated by the leadership that Niebuhr has given to such organizations as the Congress for Cultural Freedom, the Americans for Democratic Action, the Liberal party in New York State; by the profound impact of his political thinking on the State Department's Policy Planning Staff in the 1940's; by the volumes of social and political criticism that, since the mid-1920's, he has contributed to such organs of the national intelligence as the *Atlantic Monthly*, *Harper's*, the *Yale Review*, the *Sewanee Review*, the *Virginia Quarterly Review*, *Partisan Review*, the *American Scholar*, the *Nation*, the *New Republic*, the *New Leader*, and the *Reporter*; by his editorship of the fortnightly paper *Christianity and Crisis*; and by many of his books — notably *Moral Man and Immoral Society* (1932), *Christianity and Power Politics* (1940), *The Nature and Destiny of Man* (the two volumes of his Gifford Lectures, published in 1941 and 1943), *The Children of Light and the Children of Darkness* (1944), *Faith and History* (1949), *The Irony of American History* (1952), *Christian Realism and Political Problems* (1953), and *The Structure of Nations and Empires* (1959).

But, delving beneath all the rich multiplicity of theme that his thought presents, the interpreter of Niebuhr has finally to reckon with that in his work which gives body and substance to everything else, and this is the analysis of the fundamental constitution of

8

man's *humanum* — of the mysterious heights and depths of *human being* — that forms his whole sense of reality. He stands in that great line of Christian thinkers — stretching from Augustine to Pascal and from Kierkegaard to Berdyaev — whose principal preoccupation is with anthropology, with the doctrine of man. And his eminence in American cultural life is in large part a consequence of the brilliance and passion with which he has rendered the intricate tableau of man's historical existence. It is he more than anyone else who has reinstated for the intellectual community in the United States a sense of the peculiar kind of toughness and grandeur that are possible for the Christian vision. There is perhaps no other American thinker of the present time (excepting Paul Tillich, as a German *émigré*) whose work is so capable of competing for our attention with great European systematicians like Jaspers and Heidegger or with those — such as Faulkner and Camus and Sartre and Auden — who have expressed the most vital poetic vision of our period.

Though Niebuhr's thought moves most deeply within the dimension of theological anthropology, it has always been hammered out in the process of his responding to whatever presented itself as problematic in the social and political environment of his time. In this connection, one feels that the first great formative experience of his life occurred during the years in Detroit (1915-28) when, as a young parson, the blighting effect upon human life of modern industrialism, as it was manifest in the vast automobile manufactory of Henry Ford, began to focalize for him the crisis of the person in an advanced technocratic civilization. After his birth in Wright City, Missouri, in the summer of 1892, as the third son and fourth child of the Reverend Gustav Niebuhr and his wife Lydia, his boyhood was spent first in St. Charles, Missouri, and then in Lincoln, Illinois, the places where his father had the major part of his career as a pastor of the Evangelical Synod (a small Lutheran denomination which merged with a Calvinist communion in 1934 to form the Evangelical and Reformed Church, this in turn merging with the Congregationalists in 1956 to form the United Church of Christ). And then, after four years at Elmhurst College (in Elmhurst, Illinois) and three at Eden Theological Seminary in Missouri, he had two years in the Divinity School of Yale University, which awarded him the M.A. degree in the spring of 1915. So, in taking up his work that autumn as the minister of the Bethel Evangelical Church in Detroit, he was having his first encounter with life in a large industrial metropolis. And here it was, in Detroit — in the years following World War I, when the motor car industry was in the flush of its first great boom — that Niebuhr, as he confronted the Ford system, began to discover the real costs, in the worker's dehumanization, of this delightful new machine with which the world had fallen in love. The Ford administration was, to be sure, loudly trumpeting their magnanimity in having instituted a five-day week and in paying a minimum wage of five dollars a day. But they said nothing of the nervous tensions that were exacted of their workers through the cunning innovations of their efficiency experts; nor did they acknowledge the long annual periods of unemployment for which no compensation was provided out of the company's reserves of a quarter of a billion dollars. As Niebuhr has since remarked, "Ford was celebrated throughout the world as a great humanitarian and undoubtedly regarded himself as one." But he himself, as a working parson in Detroit, knew young men so broken by their labor in the automobile foundries that they had to spend the better part of their weekends in bed. And he had directly observed the appalling conditions of work in the factories. After visiting one of them he recorded his impressions in his diary (*Leaves from the Notebook of a Tamed Cynic*, 1929): "The heat was terrific. The

10

men seemed weary. Here manual labor is a drudgery and toil is slavery. The men cannot possibly find any satisfaction in their work. They simply work to make a living. Their sweat and their dull pain are part of the price paid for the fine cars we all run. . . . We all want the things which the factory produces and none of us is sensitive enough to care how much in human values the efficiency of the modern factory costs."

On Niebuhr's reckoning, the claims of the Ford people to produce a cheap car of good quality were to be granted; but, increasingly in the 1920's, he came to feel that the production of this little tin lizzie entailed a rape of human personality so brutal as to make a mockery of the moral pretensions of the Ford establishment. It is not therefore surprising that his first book, *Does Civilization Need Religion?* (1927), was a direct consequence of the reflections on the predicament of the person in a technocratic society that were induced by his Detroit experience. It is pervasively imbued with alarm at the threat of depersonalization that is posed by the fundamental structures of life in an industrial civilization. The question raised in the title of the book is answered affirmatively because "the social imagination which religion, at its best, develops upon the basis of its high evaluation of personality" makes for a profound "reverence for human personality." It was a time, he felt, when the main task of social reconstruction involved resistance against the tendency of a technocratic culture to reduce men to functions in a social process — and in such a time, he argued, the reverence for man that is fostered by the religious imagination must be acknowledged as indispensable.

But Niebuhr was already beginning to question the relevance to the modern situation of the particular forms of the religious imagination represented by liberal Protestantism. Its social idealism — as expressed in the tradition of men like Washington Gladden, Francis Peabody, Lyman Abbott, Shailer Matthews, and Wal-

11

ter Rauschenbusch — had, to be sure, voiced an authentic protest against much of the moral crudity of laissez-faire capitalism, but its overreadiness to identify the shape of its own meliorism with the Kingdom of God betrayed a "psychology of defeat" and a pathetic abrogation of the distinctive office of religion in the cultural order. For "a religion which is perfectly at home in the world has no counsel for it which the world could not gain by an easier method." When, for the sake of impressing the world with its "mundane interests," religion so secularizes itself as to become merely "a kind of harmless adornment of the moral life," then it is nothing more than a dispensable excrescence. Already in the late 1920's, Niebuhr had begun to feel that something like this kind of failure had resulted from that whole impulse in liberal Protestantism that had found its characteristic expression in the Social Gospel movement. This was a style of Christian thought that prided itself on "its bright and happy worldliness," and, in permitting its commitment to any kind of transcendent religious position to be dissipated in eagerness to transform "the natural and social environment of personality," it was by way of degenerating into merely another kind of "culture-religion" and of losing its capacity for genuinely radical criticism. "Whenever religion feels completely at home in the world," said Niebuhr, "it is the salt which has lost its savor." Yet, though his book of 1927 anticipated his later and more stringent critique of theological liberalism, it was itself, fundamentally, an expression of the ethos of the liberal movement in American Protestantism — most notably perhaps in the persistence with which it took "religion" (or something called "high religion") as its main premise, Christianity being implicitly regarded as merely one expression of the *homo religiosus*.

A year after the appearance of this first book Niebuhr resigned his Detroit pastorate and went to New York City to join the faculty of Union Theological Seminary, where he was to remain until his retirement in 1960. But his removal from a parochial ministry to an academic post was in no way accompanied by any withdrawal from the arena of social action and political debate; indeed, if there was any shift in this phase of his life, it was toward a deepening of involvement. In 1929, he was serving with Paul Douglas (then a professor at the University of Chicago, and later to become a member of the United States Senate) and John Dewey on the Executive Committee of the League for Independent Political Action; he was still active in the Fellowship of Reconciliation, the leading pacifist organization on the American scene; and, in 1930, he was founding the Fellowship of Socialist Christians and running for Congress as the candidate of the Socialist party in the Morningside Heights community of New York City. And, despite all these and other activities in public life, his restless pen was fast becoming one of the most prolific in American intellectual life.

Throughout the early years in New York Niebuhr was steadily moving toward a more radical political orientation and a more conservative theological position. These were of course years — the early 1930's — of economic stoppages and social breakdown: everywhere, despite the nation's enormous productive capacity, there was grinding poverty. And the wintry bleakness that had settled down not only on the American scene but on the larger part of the Western world brought to men the sense of being somehow utterly unprotected before the irrational hazards of life in a technological culture. It was indeed a time that found its aptest description in Yeats' lines in "The Second Coming":

> Things fall apart; the centre cannot hold;
> Mere anarchy is loosed upon the world,
> The blood-dimmed tide is loosed, and everywhere
> The ceremony of innocence is drowned;
> The best lack all conviction, while the worst
> Are full of passionate intensity.

As Niebuhr contemplated the shambles, he became deeply convinced that modern liberalism, whether in its secular or in its religious version, could not be expected to provide any relevant guidance for social and political reconstruction. The secular tradition of Locke and Jefferson and Stuart Mill and John Dewey appeared to him to be very largely the ideological expression of the characteristic utopianism of bourgeois mentality, with its faith that "the egoism of individuals is being progressively checked by the development of rationality . . . and that nothing but the continuance of this process is necessary to establish social harmony. . . ." In accordance with such a faith, social injustice is believed to have its main roots in ignorance — which must itself gradually yield before the extension of enlightenment through education and before the power of moral suasion. But to suppose that justice is guaranteed by the characters of individuals rather than social systems and, in the ordering of society, to pin one's faith on the extension of scientific intelligence is to be blinded to the living actualities of politics. For, wherever there is injustice in society, there is some significant disproportion of power, and whichever group it is that constitutes the agency of exploitation can be dislodged only when power is raised against it. By the early 1930's Niebuhr had become convinced that no realistic recognition of this fact could be expected from secular idealists whose mild Pelagianism was for him most perfectly instanced in the social philosophy of John Dewey.

Nor could he find Protestant liberalism to be any less bankrupt; in fact, by now he had come to regard it as involving little more than a reinterpretation of the Christian faith in accordance with the system of secular values descending from the Enlightenment. In its identification of the Kingdom of God with that ideal society which secular idealists expected to develop through an evolutionary process, in its belief that man's natural egoism was being

progressively checked through "the growth of a religiously inspired goodwill," in its simple confidence in the possibility of
politically incarnating the absolute imperatives of the Gospel,
in its radiant optimism about the moral plasticity of human nature, in its incorrigible habit of supposing that "if only" men
would take the Sermon on the Mount seriously, then all human
tensions would become easily manageable — in all this Niebuhr dis-
cerned what he took to be proof of the spiritual dependence of
Christian liberals upon the secular piety of bourgeois idealism.
So, in the face of the social debris of 1930, he found the Social
Gospel, with its naive preachments about the "service motive," to
be as incompetent and irrelevant as secular rationalism.

It was out of this profound exasperation with "the liberal culture of modernity" that his famous book of 1932 was written,
Moral Man and Immoral Society. And its explosive effect in American theological circles is perhaps unequaled by the impact of any
other single book of the last half-century. As the English theologian Alan Richardson recalls, it seemed, "especially to those of
the older generation, to be the outpouring of a cynical and perverse spirit, very far removed from the benevolent and sanguine
serenity which was held to be the hallmark of a truly Christian
mind." Indeed, far from laying the ground for any kind of theological reconstruction, it seemed to many of his Christian readers
that Niebuhr was destroying the very possibility of a Christian
philosophy, for, as Professor Richardson says, "their dearest as-
sumptions concerning man's perfectibility, his kinship with the
divine, his natural goodness, were [being] . . . demolished with
ruthless iconoclasm." But Niebuhr felt that Christianity could not
be relevantly related to the malaise of modern society until it as-
similated a more sophisticated understanding of the problem of
power than had been achieved by either secular or religious moralism. It was toward such a sober realism that his book was poised.

To those who proposed education and scientific intelligence as the sufficient solvent of social disorder, Niebuhr wanted to say — and chiefly to John Dewey — that "while it is possible for intelligence to increase the range of benevolent impulse . . . there are definite limits in the capacity of ordinary mortals . . . to grant to others what they claim for themselves." Men simply are not as careful of the interests of their fellows as they are of their own. And the inability of reason, however highly developed, to overcome this natural sluggishness of the moral imagination makes nonsense, he declared, of the whole theory of the "cultural lag" for which the social science of the period had such a great fondness — the notion that the achievement of social and political harmony waits only upon the development of "experimental procedures" in the common life commensurate with the experimentalism of the physical sciences. No, said Niebuhr, the natural egoism of social collectives is such that a tolerable justice can be achieved only by guaranteeing to each group enough power to counterbalance that of other groups by which it might be exploited. In short, his contention was that the ordering of society is a matter of *politics*, not of pedagogy.

And against the moralism of liberal Christianity, Niebuhr asserted that the ethic of *agape* represents "a final and absolute possibility which is, in some respects, equally distant from all political programs because all of them involve elements of coercion and resistance which are foreign to a commonwealth of pure brotherhood and love." The relevant norm, in other words, for political decision and social policy is not love but justice, not the uncoerced self-oblation of the Kingdom of God but the kind of mutuality that envisages a decent balance between the claims and counterclaims of the contending factions which constitute a dynamic society. To attempt to derive proximate social and political judgments from the absolute ethic of the Sermon on the Mount is

16

merely to indulge in a sentimental perfectionism that obscures the concrete possibilities of social reformation — which never move beyond an uneasy armistice between the demands of love and the demands of competing power blocs.

The problem, then, to which *Moral Man and Immoral Society* addressed itself was the problem of power. Its most basic contention was that, though to some extent "it may be possible . . . to establish just relations between individuals . . . purely by moral and rational suasion and accommodation," in "inter-group relations this is practically an impossibility. The relations between groups must therefore always be predominantly political rather than ethical, that is, they will be determined by the proportion of power which each group possesses at least as much as by any rational and moral appraisal of the comparative needs and claims of each group." Instead of sentimental dreaming about the "beloved community" of Protestant liberal idealism, the course of responsibility requires strict attention to the most judicious ways in which force may be deployed toward the end of securing a just distribution of power within the commonalty.

It was precisely his growing sense of the impossibility ever of discarding the tactics of force in the relations between nations and social classes that increasingly led Niebuhr in the early 1930's to doubt the cogency of pacifism. His book of 1932 makes it clear that, by this time, he had reached the point of having virtually to abandon his earlier commitment to the pacifist position. For, instead of making their witness simply as a way of disavowing the moral ambiguity inherent in all the more tentative norms of relative justice, American pacifists were in the habit of claiming the gospel of nonviolence (Christ-*cum*-Gandhi) to be a viable alternative at the level of *political* strategy. And though in 1932 Niebuhr was still somewhat uncertain about the possibility of validating international war, it had become apparent to him, at least in terms of

17

the class struggle, that the more conventional forms of pacifism were but another indication of the political incompetence of Christian liberalism, of its penchant for the purity of ideals and its distaste for the practical requirements of social strategy in a morally ambiguous world. The trouble with pacifists, he had come to feel (as he was to say a few years later to the Canadian Richard Roberts), was that they supposed they could live in history without sinning; their moral fastidiousness was too great to permit them to pit self-interest against self-interest as a way of achieving justice; and, in thus abdicating from the messiness of politics, they were in effect preparing to submit "to any demands, however unjust, and . . . to any claims, however inordinate." Men like the missionaries Kirby Page and E. Stanley Jones and the editor of the *Christian Century,* Charles Clayton Morrison, were calling this the "way of Jesus" or the "way of the Cross," but, for Reinhold Niebuhr, it was simply a way of contracting out of history.

In *Reflections on the End of an Era,* the book which appeared two years after *Moral Man and Immoral Society,* Niebuhr continued to argue the importance of developing a political theory which would be radical "not only in the realistic nature of its analysis but in its willingness to challenge the injustices of a given social system by setting power against power until a more balanced equilibrium of power is achieved." At this stage in his development, his reaction against the optimistic moralism of liberal Christianity was leading him toward Marxism, for here at least was a system into which there was built some sense of the recalcitrances of history, of the duplicitousness of which man is capable, and some realistic understanding of the dynamics of power in human affairs. The Marxist analysis of "the logic" of modern history struck him as essentially sound: he liked its apocalyptic melodramatism, its imagination of judgment and disaster, which more closely approximated, he felt, the spirit of Hebrew prophecy

18

than liberalism, either secular or religious; and he too had begun to feel that capitalism was doomed.

Though Niebuhr on occasion chose to refer to himself in the early 1930's as a "Christian Marxist," it would in fact be erroneous to regard Marxism as having had any greater importance for him than as a kind of armory that furnished additional resources of rhetoric for the critique of liberalism. His impatience with what he took to be the bumbling of the New Deal in the first eight years of the Roosevelt administration did, to be sure, confirm his misgivings during this period about the capacity of capitalism to effect any deep reform of itself — so that, in this way, he was open to Marxist pessimism about bourgeois society. It is also true that it was not until the end of the decade that the issues of foreign policy led him to see the dangerous irrelevance of the Socialist party's isolationism; it was only then that Roosevelt's crafty expedience began to represent for him, instead of mere lack of principle, precisely the kind of realistic exercise of power that he had always regarded as the hallmark of political sagacity. Many years elapsed, in other words, before Niebuhr came round to acknowledging that the kind of mixed economy and pragmatic political program that had been elaborated under the New Deal may have been "a better answer to the problems of justice in a technical age than its critics of either right or left had assumed."

But, for all of the captiousness with which he evaluated public policy in the first two terms of the Roosevelt administration, he was never in any sense a doctrinaire Marxist. Arthur Schlesinger, Jr., has brilliantly reviewed this aspect of Niebuhr's thought, reminding us of the anxiety he was expressing throughout the decade about the tendency of Communist Messianism to breed a reckless fanaticism and, through the socialization of economic power, to create an inordinate political tyranny. The Moscow trials of 1938 and the Hitler-Stalin pact of '39 were, of course, for him, as for many others, an unambiguous disclosure of the corruption at the very center of the Communist movement. And during the past twenty-five years the demonry that is inherent in both Marxist theory and Communist practice has nowhere (on either the European or the American scene) been more trenchantly exposed than in his voluminous political and theological writings.

So it is not incorrect to say that Niebuhr never had any serious illusions about Marxism. Yet its rhetoric and certain of its insights (its organic view of society, its theory of class conflict and social ideology, its definition of the problem of social injustice in terms of economic inequality) did for a time sharpen his polemic against liberalism, particularly at the point of its illusions about the possibility of simply translating ethical ideals into political actuality. It is this phase of his thought that is perhaps most apparent in *Reflections on the End of an Era*.

But, then, the very ruthlessness of Niebuhr's deflation of moralism as a style of social and political thought made it necessary that he should himself eventually attempt to restate in a constructive way the relation of ethics to politics. This was the task that he began to undertake in his book of 1935, *An Interpretation of Christian Ethics* — and particularly in the famous chapter of that book that is called "The Relevance of an Impossible Ethical Ideal." Here it was that Niebuhr's campaign against the "free-floating imperatives" — the phrase is Donald Meyer's — of Social Gospel idealism began to issue in a recovery of the doctrine of original sin, and his analysis of social and political reality thus moved into the more fundamental dimension of theological anthropology. Indeed, it would not be oversimplifying his development to say that by the mid-1930's he had truly become for the first time a theologian, his thought being now fecundated by the more emphatically distinctive insights of the Christian faith.

The essential question that is tackled in *An Interpretation of*

20

Christian Ethics is how one moves from the ethic of *agape,* with its radical perfectionism, to viable norms of ethical discrimination in the historical order. Niebuhr's contention was that the bankruptcy of both conventional orthodoxy and liberal Christianity is nowhere more in evidence than in the extent to which this problem, from both perspectives, ceases to be a real problem. For orthodoxy, in prematurely identifying the radical imperatives of faith with the myths of a prescientific age and with "canonical moral codes" of the past, abdicates from any genuine effort to make its heritage relevant to contemporary experience. Liberalism, on the other hand, in its anxiety "to prove . . . that it does not share the anachronistic ethics or believe the incredible myths of orthodox religion," has so completely adjusted what is radical in the Christian faith to "the characteristic credos and prejudices of modernity" that all the tension between "the transcendent impossibilities of the Christian ethic of love" and the immanent possibilities of the historical process has disappeared.

Niebuhr wants very much to insist that the normative element in Christian ethical thought is radically perfectionist and transcendent. For the *agape* of the Cross, in its sacrificial heedlessness and universalism, represents a degree of moral rigorism that surpasses any simple historical possibility: it makes no concessions even to the most "natural" self-regarding impulses and distances itself from every form of self-assertion, even from "the necessary prudent defenses of the self, required because of the egoism of others." The ethic of *agape* is, in short, an utterly unprudential rigorism which is impossible of fulfillment by the natural man in the immediate situations of historical existence.

Yet, as Niebuhr has consistently maintained since the appearance of his book of 1935, *agape* is the only adequate final norm of human life, because no other does full justice to the dimension of depth in which the human spirit is set. It does not, to be sure, "deal at all with the immediate moral problem of every human life — the problem of arranging some kind of armistice between various contending factions and forces. It has nothing to say about the relativities of politics and economics, nor of the necessary balances of power which exist and must exist in even the most intimate social relationships." But, then, it is the nature of man, through his radical freedom, perpetually to transcend all the cohesions that make up his communal life: he is not bound by any of them. He is, of course, "imbedded in the passing flux" of nature and history and is "the prisoner of the partial perspectives of a limited time and place." But the fact that, through reason and memory and imagination, he can surmount himself and his world indeterminately means that his life cannot find its true ground in any of the proximate norms that emerge out of historical experience, and that he is therefore driven by the inner dynamism of his nature toward a transcendent norm.

This is for Niebuhr the mark of the unique dignity of man, that, though mortal and "imbedded in the flux of finitude," he stands, by reason of his radical freedom, under ideal possibilities. But it is precisely his situation on this frontier between the temporal and the eternal, between the realm of nature and the realm of spirit, that makes possible at once everything that is noble and everything that is ignoble in the human drama. Man is always trying to "translate his finite existence into a more permanent and absolute form of existence. Ideally men seek to subject their arbitrary and contingent existence under the dominion of absolute reality. But practically they always mix the finite with the eternal and claim for themselves, their nation, their culture, or their class the center of existence. This is the root of all imperialism in man and explains why the restricted predatory impulses of the animal world are transmuted into the boundless imperial ambitions of human life." Thus it is that "devotion to every transcendent value is corrupted by the effort to insert the interests of the self into that value. The organizing center of life and history must transcend life and history, since everything which appears in time and history is too partial and incomplete to be its center. But man is destined, both by the imperfection of his knowledge and by his desire to overcome his finiteness, to make absolute claims for his partial and finite values. He tries, in short, to make himself God." And this is the root and the nature of sin.

The seat of the trouble, in other words, is not finitude itself, but finitude pretending to be something more than finite. *An Interpretation of Christian Ethics* suggests that it is just its illumination of this profound pathos of human spirituality that constitutes the genius of the classical Christian doctrine of "original sin." Niebuhr has little patience with the tendency of traditional orthodoxy so to historicize the myth of the Fall as to convert the doctrine of "original sin" into a doctrine of "inherited corruption." "If original sin is an inherited corruption, its inheritance destroys the freedom and therefore the responsibility which is basic to the conception of sin. The orthodox doctrine is therefore self-destructive." And sin is "original" only in the sense of its being pervasively and perennially characteristic of human existence.

Now this incorrigible tendency of the human creature always to claim more for himself than he ought to claim, always to mingle idealizing pretensions with his most ideal aspirations, and to accentuate "his natural will-to-live into an imperial will-to-power by the very protest which his yearning for the eternal tempts him to make against his finiteness" — this deep crookedness and duplicity of the human heart is not something that can be broken by simple rational suasion or by moralistic exhortations to "follow in His steps." The self-emptying love that is incarnate in the New Testament picture of Jesus as the Christ does indeed surpass the limit of man's moral possibilities, and to confront it is to be reduced

23

to despair. But it is precisely out of such despair that there arises "the godly sorrow which worketh repentance." And it is just here, Niebuhr suggests, that we may discern "the relevance of an impossible ethical ideal"; the law of love is, to be sure, an impossibility; yet it cannot be "relegated simply to the world of transcendence," for always "it offers immediate possibilities of a higher good in every given situation," and it is for this reason that it proves itself to be the true pinnacle of the moral imagination. A perfectionist ethic presents us, in other words, with a final norm that transcends the range of possible achievement; but, though it is never fully realized in either intention or action, it makes possible the kind of searching criticism of both intention and action that provides the impetus for the highest moral creativity.

So to conceive the relation of the sacrificial heedlessness of *agape* to the various modes of calculated mutuality that make up the realm of proximate norms and achievement is not, however, wholly to dispel the suspicion that Niebuhr's ethical thought arouses, that it does in some degree involve a very abstract kind of Kantian formalism. Though he makes frequent use of such general principles of morality as equality and justice and freedom, there is little systematic definition of precisely how it is that such "middle axioms" bring the "possibilities of a higher good" disclosed by the absolute norm of *agape* into immediate relation to the concrete issues of moral perplexity. He tends to see the ethical situation as one in which an absolute norm always makes possible a critical perspective on whatever systems of reciprocity men devise for the conduct of life. But never does he manage fully to rescue from the realm of the problematical the precise nature of the assistance that the unprudential rigorism of a perfectionist ethic offers men living in a world in which it is perilous ever to forswear prudence. It does, to be sure, offer a vision of higher "possibilities," but this hardly provides a workable canon of ethical discrimination.

24

The whole shape and direction of his argument in the book of 1935 (which was originally presented as the Rauschenbusch Memorial Lectures in the Colgate-Rochester Divinity School) made it clear that Niebuhr's social and political analysis and his debate with "the liberal culture of modernity" were gradually deepening down into a fundamental restatement of Christian theology. In its theological richness, it was his book of 1937, *Beyond Tragedy*, that made this maturing process unmistakably manifest, for here it began to be evident that his tutelage under the Fathers and the Reformers — and particularly under Augustine — was making for a brilliant recovery of the great themes of classical Christianity.

Beyond Tragedy — like the moving book that appeared in 1946, *Discerning the Signs of the Times* — is a collection of "sermonic essays" which grew out of sermons that had been preached in college and university chapels. Both books put us in mind of what a pity it is that so few of Niebuhr's sermons have reached the printed page — and these in a form representing such a systematization of the original deliverances that they have very nearly ceased to be examples of the sermon as a genre of rhetoric and have become theological essays. Niebuhr has been one of the great Christian preachers of the modern period, his only peer on the American scene perhaps having been the Presbyterian George Buttrick (till recently the dean of the Chapel of Harvard University). But his immense popularity in the great churches and university chapels of the land has never been won by way of reliance, even in the slightest degree, on the vague hyperbole and tawdry homiletical devices of the conventional sorcerer of the pulpit. Those who have faced his lucid and mercurial brilliance from the pew will surely agree that their deepest impression has been that of an enormously shrewd and worldly intelligence whose overriding interest centers in the special kind of illumination that is cast by the Christian faith upon the major perplexities of modern man. One's impression (as T. S. Eliot says of Pascal) is of a man "highly passionate and ardent, but passionate only through a powerful and regulated intellect" — who is speaking "to those who doubt, but who have the mind to conceive, and the sensibility to feel, the disorder, the futility, the meaninglessness, the mystery of life and suffering, and who can only find peace through a satisfaction of the whole being."

The basic analysis of the human situation in *Beyond Tragedy* moves very much along the same line that is taken in *An Interpretation of Christian Ethics*: "Man is mortal. That is his fate. Man pretends not to be mortal. That is his sin. Man is a creature of time and place, whose perspectives and insights are invariably conditioned by his immediate circumstances. But man is not merely the prisoner of time and place . . . He is not content to be merely American man, or Chinese man, or bourgeois man, or man of the twentieth century. He wants to be man. . . . His memory spans the ages in order that he may transcend his age. His restless mind seeks to comprehend the meaning of all cultures so that he may not be caught within the limitations of his own." Without all this "man could not come to his full estate. But it is also inevitable that these towers should be Towers of Babel, that they should pretend to reach higher than their real height; and should claim a finality which they cannot possess." In the ever wider and wider spheres of reality which he is capable of envisaging, man "knows that he ought to act so as to assume only his rightful place in the harmony of the whole. But his actual action is always informed by the ambition to make himself the centre of the whole." Thus it is that "guilt and creativity are inextricably interwoven" in human existence. Yet "Christianity does not regard the inevitability of guilt in all human creativity as inherent in the nature of human life. Sin emerges, indeed, out of freedom and is possible only because man is free; but it is done in freedom, and therefore man . . . bears responsibility for it," rather than creation or exist-

26

ence as such. The testimony of the essential goodness of creation as such is, in short, a basic affirmation of the Christian faith, for its trust is in "a good God who created a good world, though the world is not now good."

But the fact that that which contaminates the world with the poisons of sin arises out of man's freedom means that the hope of the fulfillment of life must be a hope that envisages a fulfillment beyond the possibilities of historical existence. "The possibilities of the fulfilment of this life transcend our experience not because the soul is immortal and the body is mortal but because this human life, soul and body, is both immersed in flux and above it, and because it involves itself in sin in this unique position from which there is no escape by its own powers. The fulfilment of life beyond the possibilities of this existence is a justified hope, because of our human situation, that is, because a life which knows the flux in which it stands cannot be completely a part of that flux. On the other hand this hope is not one which fulfils itself by man's own powers." God, therefore, "must complete what remains incomplete in human existence."

Yet "the Kingdom of God must still enter the world by way of the crucifixion." Though love is the law of life, "when it enters the world of relative justice and balanced egotism it is destroyed in it. The suffering servant dies on the cross." The paradox at the heart of the Christian faith arises out of the assertion that, nevertheless, in this apparently tragic fact we may discern man's deliverance from his woe. For He who dies upon the Cross, though He is God incarnate, also represents the essential nature of man, the "second Adam," as St. Paul says; and the crucifixion of the second Adam by the first Adam, in proving that human nature has deviated from its own inner law, proves also that sin is not an essential part of human nature as such. It does, to be sure, prove that "sin is so much a part of existence that sinlessness cannot maintain itself

27

in it." But it also establishes that "sin is not a necessary and inherent characteristic of life. Evil is not a part of God, nor yet a part of essential man. This Saviour is a revelation of the goodness of God and the essential goodness of man, *i.e.*, the second Adam. He is indeed defeated in history but in that very defeat proves that he cannot be ultimately defeated. That is, he reveals that it is God's nature to swallow up evil in Himself and destroy it. Life in its deepest essence is not only good but capable of destroying the evil which has been produced in it. Life is thus not at war with itself. Its energy is not in conflict with its order. Hence the Saviour truly says: 'Weep not for me.' "

Now what in part makes this book of 1937 so notable a milestone in the development of Niebuhr's thought and in twentieth-century theology is the radicalism with which it carries forward the proposal that had been made in *An Interpretation of Christian Ethics*, regarding the necessity of interpreting Christian dogma in "mythical" terms. In the earlier book he had expressed his impatience with the tendency of traditional orthodoxy so to literalize the mythical element in religious discourse as to annul what is truly dialectical in the Christian apprehension of time and eternity. The real genius of myth as a mode of thought is, as he argued there, that "it points to the timeless in time, to the ideal in the actual, but does not lift the temporal to the category of the eternal (as pantheism does), nor deny the significant glimpses of the eternal and the ideal in the temporal (as dualism does)." But traditional orthodoxy, in developing the Biblical view of reality into a rigid supernaturalist scheme of two discrete levels of being, simply achieves an obscurantist petrifaction of apprehensions whose dynamic and dialectical character ought to be preserved. So an ancillary theme in the argument of *Beyond Tragedy* concerns "the necessary and perennially valid contribution of myth to the biblical world view."

28

We are, for example, says Niebuhr, "deceivers yet true, when we say that God created the world," for this is not to account for the origin of the world in some particular and dateable moment of cosmic history; but in no other way can the mythical imagination of religious faith express its sense of the transcendent majesty of God and of the utter dependence upon Him of everything that exists. "We are deceivers, yet true, when we say that man fell into evil," for the Garden of Eden is to be found on no one's map, and the Fall is locatable on no historical calendar; but, though the myth of the Fall designates no single historical occurrence, it does in a way speak profoundly of that which is presupposed in every human action. "We are deceivers, yet true, when we affirm that God became man to redeem the world from sin. The idea of eternity entering time is intellectually absurd." Nevertheless, when Christianity speaks of God's Word having been made flesh, it is asserting that "God's word is relevant to human life"; it is declaring "that an event in history can be of such a character as to reveal the character of history itself; that without such a revelation the character of history cannot be known." And so too are we "deceivers, yet true, when we insist that the Christ who died on the cross will come again in power and glory, that he will judge the quick and the dead and will establish his Kingdom"; but in this way Christianity speaks of its belief that the human enterprise will not end tragically, and it declares that "the ground of our hope lies not in human capacity but in divine power and mercy. . . ."

This, then, is the reading of the Christian faith that Niebuhr offered in *Beyond Tragedy*. And by the late 1930's it was becoming apparent not only on the American scene but also in British and European circles that here was a gifted new presence in modern theology who had already found the authority of his own brilliant and commanding voice. At the great conference in Oxford in 1937, where the world leadership of the rapidly burgeoning ecumenical movement in non-Roman Christianity was gathered in an impressive convocation, he was a striking figure. The greeting that was uttered by William Temple (then Archbishop of York, later of Canterbury) on this occasion of their first meeting — "At last I've met the troubler of my peace" — doubtless expressed what was being felt by many of Christendom's most distinguished theologians. The word was fast getting round that Reinhold Niebuhr, along with Karl Barth and Emil Brunner and Paul Tillich, was one of the most formidable strategists of "Neo-Orthodoxy" — though the term "Neo-Orthodoxy" was never one with which he himself was happy, and it is a piece of journalistic jargon that has increasingly been rejected by many others, as a clumsy counter that distorts the actual situation in contemporary theology.

It came as no great surprise to Niebuhr's colleagues in the theological community when he was invited to the University of Edinburgh as the Gifford lecturer for the spring and autumn of 1939, an old and famous post whose only previous American incumbents had been William James, Josiah Royce, William Ernest Hocking, and John Dewey. It was in the following year that his volume *Christianity and Power Politics* appeared, a book made notable in part by the powerful critique of Christian pacifism that it presented, as the clouds of war began to hover ominously over the international horizon. But this work was quickly overshadowed by the Gifford Lectures on *The Nature and Destiny of Man*, the first volume of which, when it was published in 1941, brought the general recognition that this was Niebuhr's masterpiece.

The design of this central achievement of his career is so grandly conceived and, in its execution, is architecturally so intricate that it is impossible to produce any simple compression of the argument that gathers up and does justice to its innumerable themes. Nor is it possible in a brief essay to convey any vivid impression of that special richness of texture in the Gifford Lectures which is a result of the author's seeming to carry in his head the whole of Western intellectual tradition and to have a constantly simultaneous vision of all its myriad strands. In so curtailed an exposition as this must be, one must simply take the risk of settling upon the particular angle that affords the best view of the entire structure and, having done this, proceed then to indicate something of what is entailed in this perspective on the whole. When such rigorous concision is imposed, it would seem that the Gifford Lectures will be most fruitfully regarded as involving one of the profoundest and most original essays of the modern period in the phenomenology of selfhood. The two volumes of *The Nature and Destiny of Man* have, of course, many other dimensions: they present many startlingly fresh and acute interpretations of various phases of theological and philosophic tradition, and of movements in general intellectual and cultural history (Hellenism, Renaissance humanism, Romanticism, Marxism, etc.); and Niebuhr's own constructive theological position is extended toward a formal theory of history, a systematic Christology, and a remarkably brilliant restatement of the eschatological motifs in the Christian faith. But the decisive fulcrum is the inquiry into the nature of selfhood.

The guiding premise of Niebuhr's anthropology is grounded in a vision of human existence as composed, in its most essential character, of ambiguity. Man is, on the one hand, a creature of nature who is "unable to choose anything beyond the bounds set by the creation in which he stands": he needs air to breathe and space in which to abide; he cannot survive without the nourishment of warmth and food; yet, however abundant may be that nourishment, his life is but of short duration — and, as Pascal says, he is "engulfed in the infinite immensity of spaces . . . which know [him] not." But, though frail and subject to the contingencies of nature and history, he stands above "the structures and coherences

31

of the world," being able to order them and reorder them toward ends of his own choosing. And not only can he make the structures of nature and history the object of his own thought and the instruments of his creativity; he can also make himself the object of his thought, and even the self which thus surmounts itself — and this on into indeterminate degrees of self-transcendence.

Man is, for Niebuhr, "both free and bound, both limited and limitless." It is the necessity of recognizing this essentially ambiguous character of the human situation that provides him with the basic requirement of adequacy in terms of which he evaluates the various accounts of man's estate that are furnished by the history of culture. He finds the trouble with most of the great alternatives to the Christian faith — whether in classical rationalism or Renaissance humanism, in modern naturalism or in idealistic and romanticist philosophies — to lie in a tendency to collapse this fundamental antinomousness of human existence into some formula which either overstresses man's "dignity" and understresses his "wretchedness" or overstresses his limitation and fails sufficiently to appreciate his radical freedom. But the genius of what he calls "Biblical faith" does for him become most apparent precisely in the kind of dialectic that it maintains between its doctrine of man as creature and its doctrine of man as *imago Dei*. The contention that he argues, with great learning and rhetorical power, in book after book — but most persuasively perhaps in *The Nature and Destiny of Man* — is that "the Christian view of man is [most] sharply distinguished from all alternative views" just in the clarity with which it perceives that man belongs to *both* realms, to the realm of nature *and* to the realm of spirit.

It is, in Niebuhr's view, precisely this duality of emphasis that permits Christianity to give so profound an account of the origin and nature of sin. Its alertness to the human position as a point of juncture between nature and spirit gives it an especially acute perspective on the psychological environment in which sin becomes possible. This environing *possibility* of sin — which is "the inevitable concomitant of the paradox of freedom and finiteness in which man is involved" — Niebuhr defines as anxiety. For it is this — namely, anxiousness — which is the psychological consequence of man's being "both free and bound, both limited and limitless." And it is the analysis of anxiety in its relation to freedom and sin — with its subtle echoes, occasionally, of the similar analysis conducted in Kierkegaard's *The Concept of Dread* — that constitutes one of the most brilliantly original contributions in the first volume of the Gifford Lectures.

"Man is anxious not only because his life is limited and dependent and yet not so limited that he does not know of his limitations. He is also anxious because he does not know the limits of his possibilities. He can do nothing and regard it perfectly done, because higher possibilities are revealed in each achievement. All human actions stand under seemingly limitless possibilities. There are, of course, limits but it is difficult to gauge them from any immediate perspective. There is therefore no limit of achievement in any sphere of activity in which human history can rest with equanimity." The human condition is like that of "the sailor, climbing the mast (to use a simile), with the abyss of the waves beneath him and the 'crow's nest' above him. He is anxious about both the end toward which he strives and the abyss of nothingness into which he may fall." It is this suspension betwixt finiteness and freedom that gives rise to that sense of vertigo that induces man's profoundest dispeace. Anxiety is not itself sin; it is only the precondition of sin and the "source of temptation," to make oneself the basis of one's security or to escape from the anguish of freedom by immersing oneself in some natural vitality. But though anxiety, once conceived, tends to bring forth pride and sensuality, it does not, as the precondition of sin, make sin logically necessary: sin is committed in freedom and "can therefore not be attributed to a defect in [man's] essence. It can only be understood as a self-contradiction, made possible by the fact of his freedom but not following necessarily from it." That, says Niebuhr, is "the doctrine of original sin, stripped of literalistic illusions" — that, though sin does not necessarily follow from our human nature as such, it is nevertheless so pervasive in every moment of human existence that it seems therefore, in Kierkegaard's phrase, to "posit itself."

But, now, though human life, even in its most saintly expressions, nowhere seems to be uninfected by sin, the historical drama is by no means an affair of sheer moral anarchy. It is the Christian faith that in Christ the true meaning of history has been disclosed, that in the *agape* of the Cross the final norm of man's life has been revealed. Which means — since this norm, though disclosed, remains unfulfilled — that the actuality of man's historical existence is set within an "interim" between the First and the Second Coming of Christ; and it is to the exposition of the doctrine of history as interim that the second volume of the Gifford Lectures is very largely devoted. Here, in the interim, "sin is overcome in principle but not in fact," and thus love has "to live in history as suffering love because the power of sin makes a simple triumph of love impossible." History is not without meaning, but it presents no decisive fulfillments of its own meaning, for every realization of good is stained by the improbities of sin. Thus the New Testament hope of the *parousia*, of the suffering Messiah's coming again with "power and great glory," though it requires "demythologization," yet "embodies the very genius of the Christian idea of the historical. On the one hand it implies that eternity will fulfil and not annul the richness and variety which the temporal process has elaborated. On the other it implies that the condition of finiteness and freedom, which lies at the basis of historical existence, is a problem for which there is no solution by any human power." In short, the Christian faith reaches its ultimate pinnacle in the belief that "only the infinite pity of God is equal to the infinite pathos of human life": this is the robust confidence that lies at the heart of Niebuhr's entire thought. So one feels that the old Scotswoman had laid hold of the crux of things when, after listening to Niebuhr's lectures at the University of Edinburgh, she told him: "I dinna understand a word ye said, but somehow I ken ye were making God great."

The numerous books that Niebuhr has produced since the appearance of the two volumes of *The Nature and Destiny of Man* all represent special applications of the structure of thought that, in its main outlines, was completed by the Gifford Lectures. In 1944 his lectures on the West Foundation at Stanford University were published under the title *The Children of Light and the Children of Darkness*, and the best concise statement of Niebuhr's stratagem here is given in the book's subtitle — "A Vindication of Democracy and a Critique of Its Traditional Defence." His central thesis in this work finds perhaps its aptest summation in the famous sentence in his Preface which says: "Man's capacity for justice makes democracy possible; but man's inclination to injustice makes democracy necessary." The book is in part poised against those who, in underestimating — whether in the secular terms, say, of Hobbes or in the religious terms of Luther — man's capacity for justice, invariably tend toward some form of political absolutism. But its fiercer polemic is reserved for "the children of light," for the sentimentality of the conventional liberal democrats who "are usually foolish" because their "too consistent optimism in regard to man's ability and inclination to grant justice to his fellows obscures the perils of chaos which perennially confront every society, including a free society. . . . When this optimism is not qualified to accord with the real and complex facts of human nature and history, there is always a danger that sentimentality will give way to despair and that a too consistent optimism will alternate with a too consistent pessimism." And the unillusioned profundity with which the fortunes and misfortunes of post-Enlightenment democratic ideology are analyzed puts one in mind of the similar analysis that Camus was to undertake a few years later in *L'Homme révolté*.

The book on democracy also looks forward to the book of 1952, *The Irony of American History*, in which Dr. Niebuhr undertook a closer specification of the predicament of democratic society in terms of the American experience. Here, again, it is "the children of light" who are dealt with most critically. For theirs, he suggests, is the legacy that makes it most difficult today for America to address itself with sobriety to the troubled scene of international politics; that is to say, both New England Puritanism on the one hand and Jeffersonianism and Virginian Deism on the other have bequeathed us a spiritual heritage that induces a sense of America as God's new "Israel," as a "separated" people through whom mankind makes a new beginning. But the conviction of innocence that is thereby wrought so deeply into the nation's sense of its identity ill equips it for the exercise of power in its present position of supremacy in the world community. And the American situation is rendered particularly ironical by the fact that what we face in our chief foe (Russian communism) is very largely an intensification of many of our most characteristic values and illusions — our materialism, our preoccupation with technics, our "innocence" and self-righteousness, and our supposition that we are the masters of historical destiny. Indeed, the refutation of our forefathers' hopes that is offered by the reality of our present situation makes irony, in Niebuhr's view, the definitive category for the interpretation of American history; and we are saved, he suggests, only by the triumph of practice over dogma, only by "the ironic triumph of the wisdom of common sense over the foolishness of [our] wise men."

After the close of World War II, the rapid and terrifying intensification of Cold War politics, under the threatening specter of the big mushroom, increasingly prompted Dr. Niebuhr to explore the relevance of an eschatological faith in a period of frustration and disappointment, when "the moral and spiritual resources to achieve a just and stable society in global terms are not yet available." In the volume of "sermonic essays" called *Discerning the Signs of the Times*, which appeared in 1946, he undertook to speak of the special kind of sanity which may be the fruit of such a faith in this late, bad time.

It is, he said, an "age between the ages," when " 'one age is dead and the other is powerless to be born.' The age of absolute national sovereignty is over; but the age of international order under political instruments, powerful enough to regulate the relations of nations and to compose their competing desires, is not yet born." We are therefore a people who must learn how to live with the problem of frustration. And, in a time when contemporary history offers us nothing but "calculated risks" and disappointed hopes, we must also learn "to do our duty without allowing it to be defined by either our hopes or our fears." For "we do not know how soon and to what degree mankind will succeed in establishing a tolerable world order. Very possibly we will hover for some centuries between success and failure, in such a way that optimists and pessimists will be able to assess our achievements, or lack of them, with an equal degree of plausibility. In such a situation it is important to be more concerned with our duties than with the prospect of success in fulfilling them." But when we make the meaning of our life dependent wholly upon what we hope to accomplish tomorrow or the day after tomorrow, and when that achievement fails to be the perfect fulfillment of our highest hopes, our last state is apt to be worse than the first, the confusion of cynicism and despair having succeeded the confusion of optimism and illusion.

So, amidst the hell of global insecurity in which we live today, we shall perform our duties with the greater steadiness if we have something of the faith expressed by St. Paul when he declared: "Whether we live, we live unto the Lord; and whether we die, we die unto the Lord: whether we live therefore, or die, we are the Lord's." It is in "this final nonchalance about life and death, which includes some sense of serenity about the life and death of civilizations, that we shall find the strength for doing what we ought to do, though we know not what the day or the hour may bring forth." In a period "when our hopes so far exceed our grasp that we can not count on historic fulfillments to give completion to our life," the radicalism of an eschatological faith "may beguile a few from their immediate tasks." But those who are sober will find their steps fixed and stablished by the knowledge that "if in this life only we have hope in Christ, we are of all men most miserable." Such a peace as this "will offend both rationalists and moralists till the end of history. . . . But it alone does justice to the infinite complexities and contradictions of human existence. Within this peace all of life's creative urges may be expressed and enlarged. There is therefore no simple calm in it. It is as tumultuous as the ocean, and yet as serene as the ocean's depths, which bear the tumults and storms of the surface." And it is the only peace that will permit us to steer a steady course through the uncharted waters of life, in the difficult period to which history has committed us.

Discerning the Signs of the Times was followed, in 1949, by *Faith and History,* which more rigorously systematized many of the themes in the Gifford Lectures into a formal philosophy of history. In the intervening years, most of Dr. Niebuhr's writing — *The Irony of American History* (1952); *Christian Realism and*

Political Problems (1953); *Pious and Secular America* (1958); *The Structure of Nations and Empires* (1959) — has been concerned with the issues of politics, either in the dimension of history or formal theory or of concrete public policy. One feels that the hazards of life in the Western world during the past twenty years have increasingly brought him to something like the position that was expressed several years ago by Lionel Trilling in *The Liberal Imagination*, that our present "fate, for better or worse, is political." He has therefore wanted — in a way for which Mr. Trilling, one suspects, would have considerable sympathy — to force into the definition of politics so rich and complicated a conception of humanity as might enable our politics to be not merely a politics of survival but also a politics for the redemption and renewal of human life.

In one significant book of this period, however, he resumed and further developed that aspect of his thought which I have spoken of as the phenomenology of selfhood. Though *The Self and the Dramas of History* (1955) may bring to focus issues on which it was natural for Niebuhr to be meditating during his long and desperate illness in the early 1950's, his having been able to produce so intricately reasoned and brilliant a book after a series of small strokes provides an interesting measure, in human terms, of the man's resilience and genius. This work, in defining human selfhood in terms of man's capacity for "dialogue," reveals how deeply he has been influenced by the Jewish existentialist Martin Buber; in a manner recalling Buber's classic *I and Thou*, he too regards the life of man as a fundamentally "dialogic life," since human being is, for him, always being-in-relationship. But, whereas Buber sometimes appears to view the form of the I-Thou relation as essentially monadical, Niebuhr insists upon its conditioning by "the dramas of history"; and it is from this perspective that he analyzes the three dimensions of the dialogue in which man is constantly engaged — with himself, with his neighbors, and with God. "Man is primarily a historical creature," says Niebuhr — which means, in his view, that the self is at once determined by the necessities of nature and is yet able "to transcend not only the processes of nature but the operations of its own reason, and to stand, as it were, above the structures and coherences of the world." The self is not only patient of natural process: it is also free enough of it to create culture, though it "is not simply a creator of this new dimension, for it is also a creature of the web of events, in the creation of which it participates." Human existence is, in other words, "a compound of freedom and necessity" — which is to say that each aspect of man's "dialogic life" is historical. And the central contention of Niebuhr's book of 1955 is that the *historical* character of dialogic life is more truly and profoundly described by the poetic-dramatic categories of Biblical personalism than by classical rationalism (with its concern to submit the self to structures of ontology) or philosophic idealism (which, as in Hegel, absorbs the rough angularity of the existing self into universal mind) or romanticism (which ascribes to the realm of the organic "what is clearly a compound of nature and spirit") or modern psychology (whether in its behavioristic or Freudian versions).

Now, with the full stretch of Dr. Niebuhr's thought in view, the significance of his role in American intellectual life asks, finally, for some definition. And though his career may still be so much a part of the immediacy of the contemporary scene as to make remote the possibility of an adequately measured assessment, at least it can be said (as Arthur Schlesinger, Jr., remarked a few years ago) that here is a thinker of enormous power who has succeeded in restating the great themes of Christian theology "with such irresistible relevance to contemporary experience that even those who have no decisive faith in the supernatural find their own reading of experience and history given new and significant dimensions." He is the one American who has established his claim on that modern theological pantheon which includes such Europeans as Friedrich Schleiermacher and Albrecht Ritschl and Sören Kierkegaard and in which such distinguished contemporaries as Paul Tillich and Rudolf Bultmann and Karl Barth will also ultimately find their place. And — excepting possibly Kierkegaard (whose posthumous reputation is a development of our own period) and Paul Tillich, whose influence begins also to be widely felt — there is no other Christian theologian of the modern period whose work has exerted so profound an impact upon secular intellectual life. This is perhaps most immediately measurable in the field of political thought, where, as Hans Morgenthau says, he is our "greatest living political philosopher, perhaps the only creative political philosopher [in American thought] since Calhoun." This is a judgment which Professor Morgenthau and many others are prepared to make not merely because of the immense volume of brilliant analysis of the concrete issues of contemporary politics that Niebuhr has produced over the past thirty years. On most of the major social and political questions in our domestic life and, particularly since the close of World War II, on the fundamental issues of foreign policy he has, of course, produced a body of comment that has been powerfully influential in the thinking of many of the ablest journalists and theoreticians and architects of public policy in this country. But his eminence in the realm of political thought, as Professor Morgenthau rightly suggests, is more centrally a result of the kind of awareness that he — more than any other American thinker of our time — has promoted of the essentially "tragic character of the political act."

Dr. Niebuhr is occasionally charged by his colleagues in the theological community with being too much inclined, in his political thinking, toward a kind of rough-and-ready pragmatism that is insufficiently controlled by moral and theological principle — or by what they sometimes heavily denominate as "vision." But he knows that, though that balancing of claims and counterclaims by which justice is achieved can never provide the absolute norm of a social ethic, there is — short of disavowing our historical responsibilities — no escaping our involvement in these morally ambiguous pressures. He also knows that, however much "vision" may accord a certain slender dignity to our politics, the dynamism of history is such that the consequences of political action have a way of outrunning both the intent that prompted the act and any capacity that might have been mustered to foresee those consequences — so that, for the responsible man, there is no deliverance from the rough-and-ready expedience of pragmatic realism. In his strong sense of what he likes to call the "indeterminate possibilities" of history, he does indeed put us in mind of William James and his vision of the universe as open and dynamic; and, in his commitment, at the level of political methodology, to a radically empiricist experimentalism, he is, for all of the antagonism that he expressed in earlier years, not far removed from John Dewey. So, in terms of American cultural tradition, in his profound concern to invest Christianity with relevance for the social and political order, he is to be seen as an heir of the Social Gospel, despite his early rejection of its tendency to identify Christianity with the religion of progress; and, despite the polemical way in which he has frequently faced many of its chief representatives in American philosophy, he is also to be seen as an heir of pragmatism.

Though he gives short shrift to "the new conservatives," their fondness for quoting Edmund Burke does not blind him to the wisdom in Burke's view of politics as the art of the possible. Nor can he ever forget that, however many new possibilities for the realization of good each new development in history may bring, it also brings new hazards corresponding to these new possibilities — so that (as he says in the second volume of *The Nature and Destiny of Man*) "the new level of historic achievement offers us no emancipation from contradictions and ambiguities to which all life in history is subject." History, in other words, "is not its own redeemer. The 'long run' of it is no more redemptive in the ultimate sense than the 'short run.' " And thus it is that the choices which we make are never choices which have any chance of achieving a final settlement of the human problem: the peace of the *civitas terrena* is always an uneasy peace, and, as a consequence, in one of its dimensions, politics is, in its very nature, something essentially tragic.

But then, of course, to define Dr. Niebuhr's importance in secular intellectual life as having consisted in part in his reinstatement of a sense of what is tragic in political existence is to be reminded that here is indeed the basic emphasis not only of his political thought but of his total account of what André Malraux has taught us to speak of as *la condition humaine*. For radical as his commitment is to the Christian faith, and profound as his explication of its message has been, he has never lost his fidelity to what Unamuno called "the tragic sense of life." It is doubtless in this aspect of his vision that the literary community has found its most congenial access to his work. Here, the extent and depth of his influence — though widely observed — are more difficult to measure than in the field of social and political thought. His presence as a shaping force in American literary life is something that is more often conveyed in the nuances of stress and intonation than in the form of documented reference. The late F. O. Matthiessen, for example, in his European journal of 1947, *From the Heart of Europe* (published in 1948), acknowledging Niebuhr's great influence on himself, gives a clear hint of what lay behind his own powerful critique of "the nineteenth-century belief in every man as his own Messiah" in *American Renaissance*. Or, again, one suspects that the kind of stringently critical assessment of liberalism that Lionel Trilling was conducting in the 1940's owes something, in part, to the current of ideas which have been seminally present in our time in Reinhold Niebuhr. And his influence can be felt not only in contemporary criticism but also in the realm of our creative literature as well — as, for example, in the trenchant reassessment of Jeffersonian liberalism in Robert Penn Warren's *Brother to Dragons* (with its likeness, in its basic ideas, to *The Children of Light and the Children of Darkness*) or of a later, Stevensonian (?) liberalism in Frederick Buechner's fine novel of 1958, *The Return of Ansel Gibbs* (written after Buechner had had a period of study under Niebuhr at Union Seminary).

That, outside theological circles, Niebuhr's wider influence on the American cultural scene today should be felt as that of an eloquent spokesman for "the tragic sense of life" does, however, put us in mind of what may be the chief inadequacy in his work as a Christian theologian. And this is related to the earlier observation that was made of his inability, finally, to overcome in a really satisfactory way the disjunction in his ethical thinking between the *agape* of Christ and the various forms of mutuality in human relations that are the aim of all concrete ethical decision in the historical order. The sacrificial love of Christ is, in Niebuhr's view, a love which transcends all considerations of reciprocity and is therefore "beyond history," since historical existence is, perennially, a matter of adjusting the claims and counterclaims which men bring to one another in all the relations of life. Now, to be sure, this absolute norm furnishes a vantage point from which complacency about any particular system of mutuality can be criticized. But he has never succeeded in making really clear precisely how it is that the *agape* of Christ which is "beyond history" affords a way of concretely taking account of all the quandaries which men face in attempting to build systems of reciprocity that

44

are just and humane. The fundamental issue here is, of course, one which concerns the way in which the order of grace becomes effectually operative in history. But it is just at this point — where the logic of his task as a Christian theologian requires him to indicate what is involved in the whole drama of redemption — that Dr. Niebuhr is least satisfactory. He has a genius for setting forth the kind of critical pressure that the Christian doctrine of man exerts on many of the characteristic forms of modern thought. But, as one of his critics, Paul Lehmann, has suggested, "the Cross, which is apprehended and interpreted as the *basis* of a new wisdom and power, is not adequately apprehended and interpreted as *operative* wisdom and power." Which is to say that there is no systematic specification of how it is, in the perspective of Christian faith, that God actually renews and transforms human life. And this vagueness which characterizes his rendering of the doctrine of redemption is of a piece with his failure to develop systematically the doctrines of the Holy Spirit and of the Church (which Christianity has classically regarded as that extension of the Incarnation whereby God continues the atoning work that was begun in Christ).

But, though Dr. Niebuhr's rendering of the great themes of the Christian faith is in certain respects unfinished and incomplete, he has yet clarified with a singular power the continuing vitality of Reformation Christianity and the possibilities for cogent interpretation of modern experience that are still resident in its basic message. Perhaps no other native American thinker of the contemporary period has invested a Christian position with such relevance to the political and general intellectual situation of our time; and, as a consequence, his career is among the most eminent in that forum of thought which gives to the nation today its most creative engagements.

⤳ Selected Bibliography

For the period up to 1954, the definitive checklist of Dr. Niebuhr's writings is to be found in *Reinhold Niebuhr's Works: A Bibliography*, by D. B. Robertson (Berea, Ky.: Berea College Press, 1954). Professor Robertson's bibliography is particularly valuable as a guide to the hundreds of articles that Niebuhr has contributed to American journals in the years since he published his first pieces in the *Atlantic Monthly* in 1916.

Principal Works of Reinhold Niebuhr

Does Civilization Need Religion? — *A Study in the Social Resources and Limitations of Religion in Modern Life*. New York: Macmillan, 1927.

Leaves from the Notebook of a Tamed Cynic. Chicago: Willett, Clark and Colby, 1929.

The Contribution of Religion to Social Work. New York: Columbia University Press, 1932.

Moral Man and Immoral Society: A Study in Ethics and Politics. New York: Scribner's, 1932.

Reflections on the End of an Era. New York: Scribner's, 1934.

An Interpretation of Christian Ethics. New York: Harper, 1935.

Beyond Tragedy: Essays on the Christian Interpretation of History. New York: Scribner's, 1937.

Christianity and Power Politics. New York: Scribner's, 1940.

The Nature and Destiny of Man: A Christian Interpretation. Vol. I, *Human Nature*. New York: Scribner's, 1941. Vol. II, *Human Destiny*. New York: Scribner's, 1943. (Since 1949, Scribner's has been making available a one-volume edition of these Gifford Lectures.)

The Children of Light and the Children of Darkness: A Vindication of Democracy and a Critique of Its Traditional Defence. New York: Scribner's, 1944.

Discerning the Signs of the Times: Sermons for Today and Tomorrow. New York: Scribner's, 1946.

Faith and History: A Comparison of Christian and Modern Views of History. New York: Scribner's, 1949.

The Irony of American History. New York: Scribner's, 1952.

Christian Realism and Political Problems. New York: Scribner's, 1953.

46

The Self and the Dramas of History. New York: Scribner's, 1955.

Love and Justice, edited by D. B. Robertson. Philadelphia: Westminster Press, 1957.

The Godly and the Ungodly: Essays on the Religious and Secular Dimensions of Modern Life. London: Faber and Faber, 1958.

Pious and Secular America. New York: Scribner's, 1958.

Essays in Applied Christianity, edited by D. B. Robertson. New York: Meridian Books (World), 1959.

The Structure of Nations and Empires: A Study of the Recurring Patterns and Problems of the Political Order in Relation to the Unique Problems of the Nuclear Age. New York: Scribner's, 1959.

Reinhold Niebuhr on Politics, edited by Harry R. Davis and Robert C. Good. New York: Scribner's, 1960.

A Nation So Conceived: Reflections on the History of America from Its Early Visions to Its Present Power, with Alan Heimert. New York: Scribner's, 1963.

Current American Reprints

Beyond Tragedy. New York: Scribner Library. $1.45.

The Children of Light and the Children of Darkness. New York: Scribner Library. $1.25.

An Interpretation of Christian Ethics. Cleveland: Meridian Books (World). $1.25.

The Irony of American History. New York: Scribner Library. $1.25.

Leaves from the Notebook of a Tamed Cynic. Cleveland: Meridian Books. $1.35.

Moral Man and Immoral Society. New York: Scribner Library. $1.45.

Critical and Biographical Studies

Allen, E. L. *A Guide to the Thought of Reinhold Niebuhr.* London: Hodder and Stoughton, n.d.

Bingham, June. *Courage to Change: An Introduction to the Life and Thought of Reinhold Niebuhr.* New York: Scribner's, 1961.

Carnell, Edward J. *The Theology of Reinhold Niebuhr.* Grand Rapids, Mich.: W. B. Eerdmans Publishing Co., 1951.

Davies, D. R. *Reinhold Niebuhr: Prophet from America.* London: James Clarke, 1945.

Hammar, George. *Christian Realism in Contemporary American Theology: A Study of Reinhold Niebuhr, W. M. Horton, and H. P. Van Dusen.* Uppsala, Sweden: A.-B. Lundequistska Bokhandeln, 1940.

Harland, Gordon. *The Thought of Reinhold Niebuhr.* New York: Oxford University Press, 1960.

Hofmann, Hans. *The Theology of Reinhold Niebuhr,* translated by Louise Pettibone Smith. New York: Scribner's, 1956.

Kegley, Charles W., and Robert W. Bretall, eds. *Reinhold Niebuhr: His Religious, Social, and Political Thought.* Vol. II of The Library of Living Theology. New York: Macmillan, 1956. (Includes essays by Emil Brunner, Paul Tillich, John C. Bennett, Paul Ramsey, Arthur Schlesinger, Jr., Kenneth Thompson, Richard Kroner, Daniel D. Williams, Alan Richardson, William John Wolf, Paul Lehmann, and others.)

Landon, Harold R., ed. *Reinhold Niebuhr: A Prophetic Voice in Our Time.* "Essays in Tribute" by Paul Tillich, John C. Bennett, and Hans J. Morgenthau. Greenwich, Conn.: Seabury Press, 1962.

Meyer, Donald B. *The Protestant Search for Political Realism, 1919–1941.* Berkeley and Los Angeles: University of California Press, 1960. See especially Chapters XIII and XIV.

Thelen, Mary Frances. *Man as Sinner in Contemporary American Realistic Theology.* New York: King's Crown Press, 1946.

Vignaux, Georgette P. *La théologie de l'histoire chez Reinhold Niebuhr.* Neuchâtel: Delachaux & Niestlé, 1957.